D1482801

THE EFFECTS OF ECONOMIC ADJUSTMENT ON POVERTY IN MEXICO

For Joseph and Noreen Kelly

The Effects of Economic Adjustment on Poverty in Mexico

THOMAS J. KELLY
Middlebury College, Vermont

Ashgate

Aldershot • Brookfield USA • Singapore • Sydney

Published by
Ashgate Publishing Ltd
Gower House
Croft Road
Aldershot
Hants GU11 3HR
England

Ashgate Publishing Company
Old Post Road
Brookfield
Vermont 05036
USA

British Library Cataloguing in Publication Data
Kelly, Thomas J.
  The effects of economic adjustment on poverty in Mexico
  1. Economic stabilization - Mexico 2. Poor - Mexico 3. Mexico
  - Economic conditions - 1982-1994
  I. Title
  339.5'0972

Library of Congress Catalog Card Number: 99-72847

ISBN 1 84014 828 4

Printed and bound by Athenaeum Press, Ltd.,
Gateshead, Tyne & Wear.

Contents

List of Figures

List of Tables

Foreword

This study of *Economic Adjustment and Poverty in Mexico* contains numerous insights and valuable lessons for analysts and policy makers alike. Mexico's policies in the 1970s are a classic example of economic mismanagement. The country borrowed heavily during the oil boom of the late 1970s, anticipating that it could service its foreign debt from oil revenues which were expected to grow indefinitely. When the world economy went into recession in the early 1980s the country was caught off-guard by sharply rising real interest rates, a decline in its external terms of trade, a fall in export demand and a decline in foreign lending. In 1982 Mexico simultaneously experienced a debt crisis and the beginning of a long decline in living standards.

Mexico's response to the external and internal crises - structural adjustment - also was classic, namely, devaluation of the exchange rate; a dramatic reduction in public expenditure, especially public investment; trade liberalization, notably the reduction of quantitative controls over imports; privatization of state owned enterprises; and finally, in 1994, the creation with Canada and the United States of the North American Free Trade Area (NAFTA). The results of these classic structural adjustment policies were decidedly mixed, as Thomas Kelly makes clear in this excellent monograph.

In the end and after much travail the adjustment programs did succeed in reducing the rate of inflation, bringing the public sector deficit under control and altering the structure of incentives. Economic growth fell sharply and average income in 1996 still was below the level achieved in 1981, the year before the debt crisis. Public investment was slashed, falling in real terms by more than 80 per cent between 1981 and 1995, and in consequence aggregate growth rates were reduced, sectoral restructuring was made more difficult and (because public investment is the key to agricultural performance) poverty was accentuated.

Household expenditure declined less than income because the burden of adjustment fell disproportionately on savings. Between 1982 and 1993 the savings rate in Mexico collapsed, falling from 14.9 per cent to 6.4 per cent. This helped, at least in the short run, to temper the rise in poverty. Using national income and expenditure surveys for four years (1984, 1989, 1992 and 1994), Thomas Kelly shows that over the entire period the number of people living in "extreme poverty" increased by 5 million, i.e., from 13 million in 1984 (two years after the onset of the crisis) to 18 million in 1994. The incidence and intensity of extreme poverty were much greater in the rural than in the urban areas and the differences tended to increase during the decade under study.

Structural adjustment and falling output were accompanied by increased inequality. The World Bank estimates that by 1992 the Gini coefficient of expenditure was 50.3. Dr. Kelly argues, however, that at the national level, changes in average expenditure were more important in accounting for the increase in poverty than was the change in the distribution of expenditure. Within sectors, in contrast, increased inequality does help to explain the rise in poverty. The real wages of public sector employees were reduced substantially. In the private sector wage inequality also increased, with the real wages of low skilled workers falling more rapidly than the wages of skilled workers. The decline in the demand for labor was not reflected in a dramatic rise in the rate of unemployment; instead there was a shift to employment in the informal sector, where wages are lower, part-time working common and job security absent. Trade liberalization, contrary to expectations, did not lead to a net rise in employment and reduction in poverty. The reason is that capital intensive, export oriented manufacturing gained from liberalization at the expense of labor intensive enterprises oriented toward the domestic market. In agriculture, state support and the internal terms of trade moved against basic food crops (which the poor produce) whereas other crops fared relatively better.

Thus the simple, classical prescriptions for structural adjustment did not succeed in Mexico, or at best succeeded only partially. Growth was retarded, not accelerated; inequality rose rather than fell; poverty increased rather than declined; informalization of the economy occurred rather than modernization. Mexico's story needs to be better known and this book is a good place to begin.

Keith Griffin

Acknowledgements

The research presented here owes a large intellectual debt to Keith Griffin and Azizur Rhaman Khan. Their insights have done much to shape this analysis and to improve my understanding of developing economies. I am grateful for their patient guidance and support.

I would like to thank Steven Helfand for his careful reading of the manuscript and his helpful comments and discussion. Discussions with Patrick Mason, Bob Breunig, Craig Gundersen, Nilanjana Roy and Mwangi wa Githinji were critical in helping to make the empirical work in this study more precise. Diana Alarcón patiently fielded dozens of questions on the Mexican economy and the Encuesta Nacional de Ingreso-Gasto de los Hogares. Mwangi wa Githinji and James Ssemakula were instrumental in helping me to overcome programming and data handling problems. Discussions with Juan Vicente Palerm improved my understanding of the complexity of the Mexican agricultural sector.

I would like to acknowledge the assistance of el Lic. Germán Zárate-Hoyos and the Statistics Department of the Colegio de la Frontera Norte in obtaining data from the Instituto Nacional de Estadístico Geografía e Informática. Adriaan Ten Kate generously provided me with unpublished data from the Secretaría de Comercio y Fomento Industrial. I am indebted to Juan Jiménez-Osornio for allowing me time to conduct research which led to this monograph during my stay at the Departamento de Manejo y Conservación de Recursos Naturales Tropicales of the Universidad Autónoma de Yucatán.

I would like to thank Kathryn Kelly for her assistance in research carried out at The Catholic University of America and for helping to smooth my prose. I would also like to thank Kate Kelly Musica for her assistance in the preparation of the final version of the manuscript.

Financial support was provided by the Switzer Foundation, the Ford Foundation, and the University of California.

1 Introduction

This study examines how the poor were affected during the period of economic adjustment in Mexico in the 1980s and early 1990s. The experience of Mexico with adjustment began shortly after its suspension of debt repayments in 1982. The Mexican economy suffered greatly from the effects of the adjustment policies and external shocks which occurred in the early 1980s, but by the early 1990s, moderate growth had returned and Mexico was viewed as a model of economic reform worthy of imitation by other nations. However, even before the peso crisis of 1994, the high social costs associated with adjustment caused many critics to question the status of Mexico as a model of reform. The decline in real wage rates and the reduction in expenditure on social services suggested that increased poverty was a consequence of reform. This study seeks to determine if poverty did, in fact, increase during the adjustment period.

Over the course of the 1980s and early 1990s, most developing countries underwent some type of macroeconomic adjustment. In the 1970s, Chile was the sole reformer in Latin America, but by the early 1990s, almost all Latin American countries and over thirty Sub-Saharan African countries had implemented adjustment programs.

The programs were first adopted in order to correct the macroeconomic imbalances which had developed in the early 1980s and to generate higher levels of long term growth (ILO). The imbalances were due, in part, to the external shocks of unprecedented severity which affected most developing countries: their terms of trade declined, oil prices increased, interest rates soared, and the demand for their exports fell. When external financing of the imbalances was no longer available, the highly indebted countries were forced to stop borrowing and begin debt repayment. The scale of the adjustment was also unprecedented. In Latin America, the average trade deficit was four percent of GDP in 1980, and by the end of the decade the average was a 4.6 per cent surplus. This implies that aggregate demand was reduced by nearly nine percent with respect to aggregate supply (Morley).

Over the course of the 1980s and early 1990s, most adjusting countries also experienced a stagnation of their economies. Growth in per capita GDP slowed or became negative, unemployment increased, and progress in improving rates of infant mortality and educational attainment

1

slowed. This poor performance during the adjustment period followed a long period of declining poverty throughout much of the developing world and has given rise to concern about the distributional consequences of adjustment.

The primary criticisms of the adjustment programs are that the poor have been especially hard hit by the transitional costs associated with the changes in macroeconomic policy, particularly when the transitions cannot be achieved as quickly as planned; that the programs have not generally generated the growth they were designed to achieve; and that when they have generated growth, the poor have not shared in the rewards of this growth.

Despite evidence that poverty appears to have increased in many adjusting countries, it is important to note, however, that welfare levels did not fall in all adjusting countries. Colombia, Indonesia, and Côte d'Ivoire are important examples of countries which succeeded in reducing poverty during adjustment programs (Morley; Ravallion and Huppi; Demery and Squire). Furthermore, even in countries which were not so fortunate, the coincidence of rising poverty and the implementation of adjustment policies does not necessarily imply that the policy changes caused the increase in poverty. In most countries, exogenous shocks and the imbalances which made adjustment necessary were part of the cause. In addition to these complicating factors, there are difficult methodological problems involved in determining how poverty is affected by adjustment; it is impossible, for instance, to know how poverty rates would have behaved in the absence of adjustment.

The way in which adjustment policies affect poverty is, thus, the subject of vigorous debate. The debate on adjustment's effect on poverty has included a variety of theoretical and empirical approaches which have provided some basic understanding of how the various constituent parts of an adjustment program are likely to affect poverty. One of the primary conclusions of this literature is, however, that similar changes in macroeconomic policy can produce different results in different countries, depending on the initial conditions and other specific circumstances of the country in which they are applied. The fact that generalizations about the effect of adjustment on poverty cannot be universally applied highlights the importance of information on the experiences of individual nations. Given its status as a model reformer, the experience of Mexico is of particular importance.

This study examines the evolution of poverty rates in Mexico using a series of income-expenditure surveys which were administered during the adjustment period. The existence of these surveys offers an important advantage which most empirical studies of the effect of adjustment on poverty have not enjoyed. Most empirical studies have been forced to base their conclusions on inferences drawn from changes in per capita income, or employment and wage rates in the formal sector. Drawing inferences in this way may well understate the change in poverty by not taking changes in income distribution into consideration and by ignoring changes in the informal sector. In Mexico, however, the existence of high quality micro-level data on household income and expenditure from these surveys provides an unusual opportunity to measure directly how the rate of poverty has changed over the adjustment period.

The second chapter of this study explores the issue of why the adjustment policies which were administered in the 1980s and early 1990s might be expected to have an effect on poverty. The third chapter reviews the circumstances which precipitated Mexico's need for adjustment and traces the evolution of the adjustment policies which were implemented. The fourth chapter uses a number of poverty measures to estimate how poverty rates changed during the adjustment period. The fifth chapter examines the causes for the observed changes in the poverty rates. The final chapter draws some conclusions on Mexico's experience with adjustment and how the changes brought about by adjustment are likely to affect poverty rates in the future.

2   Adjustment's Impact on Poverty

This chapter examines the reasons why the adjustment policies adopted by developing countries may be expected to have an effect on the rate of poverty.   The chapter begins by reviewing the causes for the macroeconomic imbalances which made adjustment necessary and detailing the content of the stabilization and structural adjustment policies which were implemented to correct the imbalances.   The next section discusses the methodological difficulties which are inherent to the study of adjustment's effect on poverty.   The final section examines the different theoretical and empirical approaches which have been employed in the study of adjustment's effect on poverty.

Macroeconomic Imbalances

The origin of the macroeconomic imbalances which plagued many LDCs in the early 1980s may be traced to the oil price shocks of the 1970s.   The sharp increases in the prices of oil in 1973 and 1979 led to large balance of payment deficits in oil-importing LDCs.   In order to finance these balance of payments deficits, many oil-importing LDCs borrowed heavily from commercial banks.   The large inflows of foreign lending allowed these countries to avoid adjustment and to maintain consumption and investment rates comparable to the pre-shock levels.

Many LDCs thus entered the 1980s with large external account deficits and growing foreign debt.   At the same time, many LDCs were developing large fiscal deficits.   These internal imbalances were closely associated with the external imbalances as higher interest rates and a decrease in foreign lending drove fiscal deficits higher.   These fiscal deficits were often financed by monetary expansion and so were accompanied by an acceleration of inflation.

These imbalances were sustainable as long as the prevailing international economic conditions remained favorable and the commercial banks were willing to finance them.   The imbalances became unsustainable when, in the early 1980s, international economic conditions

4

changed dramatically: interest rates rose sharply, the terms of trade for LDCs declined sharply, and the demand for LDC exports fell due to a recession in the developed countries (Khan, 1993). In the case of Mexico, the balance of payments deficit grew rapidly, and when Mexico declared a moratorium on its debt service in 1982, commercial banks abruptly stopped issuing new loans to finance the imbalance.

The structure of trade for the heavily indebted LDCs was no longer tenable. Any economy with non-transitory imbalances in its external accounts must eventually adjust. The adjustment can occur automatically through income and monetary effects or can be achieved through the introduction of policy reforms (Streeten, 1989b). The advantage of implementing policy reforms is that they may be designed not only to correct macroeconomic imbalances, but also to achieve other objectives, like faster and more sustainable growth (Cornia).

When the balance of payments deficits grew and inflows of private savings stopped in the early 1980s, most LDCs chose to adjust through a set of policy reforms designed by the international financial institutions. These policy reforms, generally referred to as adjustment policies, sought to correct unsustainable macroeconomic imbalances in the economy and to change the structure of the economy in order to achieve a higher rate of long run growth (Glewwe and de Tray).

The adjustment policies include both stabilization and structural adjustment policies. Stabilization policies rely primarily on demand restraint in order to reduce the imbalances in the external account and domestic budget. A combination of deflationary policies, including wage restraint, a tighter money supply, decreased public spending, and a reduced credit ceiling, are designed to improve the balance of trade in the short run by decreasing the demand for exportable goods and imports.

Structural adjustment policies are designed to increase the efficiency of resource use in order to promote faster growth and improve the balance of trade over the medium term. The polices consist of a varying mix of expenditure switching policies and institutional and policy reforms (Lustig, 1995). The expenditure switching policies are designed to switch resources to the production of tradables and consist of real exchange rate devaluations, trade interventions, and changes in tax and pricing policies. The institutional and policy reforms are designed to increase efficiency through a greater reliance on the market and price signals. The reforms include trade liberalization, privatization, fiscal reform, financial reform, and a decrease in the size of the public sector.

Methodological Approaches to the Study of Adjustment and Poverty

Analyzing the effect of adjustment policies on poverty presents a series of difficult methodological problems. The most obvious of these is our ignorance of how the economy would have performed if the policies in question had not been undertaken. The true counterfactual, that is, the situation which would have prevailed if different policies had been chosen, cannot be known. For this reason, it can never be said definitively that some alternative policy would have yielded better results. Nor can it be said to what extent observed changes in economic variables are due to observed changes in policy. The changes in the economic variables may be due to factors which are exogenous to the analysis. In the case of adjustment programs, changes in income and employment might be due to exogenous shocks or disequilibria which existed before adjustment policies were undertaken.

Of course this problem is not unique to the analysis of adjustment policies - it is inherent to the analysis of any economic policy. However, while inferring causality between changes in policy and changes in economic variables may be misleading in any policy analysis, a number of factors combine to make the analysis of adjustment programs particularly difficult. First, it is very difficult to distinguish between the effect of adjustment programs and the exogenous shocks, economic crises, and large inflows of foreign resources which accompany the adjustment programs (Haddad, *et al.*). Second, adjustment programs are composed of a complex combination of policies whose net effects are likely to vary significantly according to the timing, sequencing, and intensity of the various components. Finally, to further complicate the analysis, policies are rarely implemented as designed. In implementation, the scope, sequencing and speed of policy reform typically vary from the project design, and partial, rather than full, implementation of the program is the norm.

Authors attempting to assess the effect of adjustment policies on poverty have employed both theoretical and empirical approaches to the problem. The theoretical studies typically employ partial equilibrium analysis designed to determine the likely results of specific policies which comprise adjustment programs. These studies are useful in identifying *a priori* the likely effects of particular policies, but the analysis is complicated by the fact that the adjustment programs typically involve a complex mix of different policies (Cornia). These different policies may affect income and employment in different ways and at different times, and they create complicated concurrent and lagged interactions whose net effect is difficult to predict (Behrman and Deolalikar). A partial solution to this methodological problem is the categorization of policy instruments with broadly similar effects into distinct groups. Cornia divides the various policy instruments associated with adjustment into three broad categories: expenditure reduction, expenditure switching, and institutional reform. Given these divisions, an attempt is made to predict the net effect of adjustment programs based on the relative weight particular programs give to the different categories.

The empirical studies are based on the notion that in order to determine how adjustment affects income and employment, a hypothetical counterfactual must be specified to establish some notion of what would have happened under alternative policies. The hypothetical counterfactual should allow for the comparison of the performance of key welfare indicators, *viz.*, employment, wages, per capita income. Most empirical studies have sought to establish an appropriate counterfactual result by generating model-based simulations. Computable general equilibrium models which include features of traditional macroeconomic models allow researchers to examine the microeconomic effects of adjustment policies on income and employment (Morrisson). These models attempt to take account of the complicated concurrent and lagged interactions which the partial equilibrium analyses cannot (Behrman and Deolalikar). There are two primary difficulties with relying on these models to carry out the empirical analysis of adjustment policies. The first is that such models have rather extreme data requirements and are simply not available for most economies. The second is that the choice of the alternative policies can be problematic. This choice is fundamental to the study. A relatively minor difference in the mix and timing of policies to be simulated may yield significantly different results. Divining what this precise mix and timing *might have been* is a rather shaky foundation on which to build the case for or against the policies which were in fact followed.

A second approach used to establish a hypothetical counterfactual is the comparison of the performance of countries which have adopted adjustment policies with the performance of countries which have not (Demery and Squire). This approach effectively treats the non-adjusting countries as controls: their performance is assumed to reveal what the performance of the adjusting countries would have been if they had not implemented an adjustment program.

The comparative approach avoids the problems associated with model-based simulations, but is limited by the extent to which the non-adjusting countries may be treated as true controls. Countries are typically selected for inclusion in the control group based on their similarity to adjusting countries; the most common criteria seem to be some measure of their economic openness, income level, and geographic region. However, despite these similarities, there may exist significant differences in economic structure which would imply quite different responses to policy changes. For example, national differences in the composition of exports or the strength of the labor movement would mean that the response of income and employment would be likely to differ as well.

The final empirical approach is the examination of welfare indicators before and after the implementation of adjustment policies (Morley, 1995; Fiszbein and Psacharopoulos). These studies seek to determine what happened to welfare levels of the poor without attempting to formalize the causal links between the adjustment programs and the economic variables they influence. This approach avoids both the problems associated with the model-based approach and the difficulties of identifying an appropriate control in cross country comparisons. The primary difficulty with these studies is that the results tend to be sensitive to the selection of the time period. Dramatic short run changes in economic variables are common in adjusting countries and so great care is required in drawing any conclusions from a single data point. It is especially difficult to select an appropriate starting point for such studies as welfare levels in the years immediately prior to the crisis are likely to have been unsustainably high.

Theoretical Approaches

The Effects of Expenditure Reduction

Expenditure reduction policies are designed to correct the trade imbalance by reducing aggregate demand and also to correct the domestic fiscal imbalance. In general, the effect of these policies will be contractionary. The precise effect on income and employment will depend on whether the fiscal balance is pursued through increasing taxes, or decreasing recurrent expenditure or investment.

The decrease of public investment will tend to decrease growth in the medium and long run. Arguments that public investment crowds out private investment are unconvincing in the context of developing economies where the complementary effects between public and private investment are typically strong (Pastor and Conroy). The decrease in public investment will be particularly harmful to the undercapitalized sectors of the economy which would benefit most from new investment. In most LDCs, the agricultural sector is undercapitalized and the loss of public investment in transportation, storage, and productivity increasing infrastructure, like irrigation, will mean lower agricultural incomes in the medium and long run.

Increasing taxes and decreasing recurrent expenditure will have a more immediate contractionary effect on the economy. These contractionary policies will tend to decrease income and employment throughout the economy. Unless accompanied by a shift toward a more equitable distribution of income, the decline in per capita income will increase poverty. While it is possible that the poor could be sheltered from the negative effects of a decrease in per capita income by an improvement in the income distribution, such a change seems unlikely to occur unless policies which are specifically designed to redistribute income accompany the expenditure reduction.

Moreover, Pastor and Dymski (1991) argue that, in the absence of redistributive policies, there are reasons to expect income distribution to worsen as a result of expenditure reduction. Pastor and Dymski base their argument on the fact that the functional distribution of income is determined in part by the relative power of capital and labor. In the case of labor, power is derived from the ability to withdraw from the production process. As the reduction in public expenditure slows economic growth, the scarcity of labor will decrease, and it will become less feasible for workers to voluntarily withdraw from production. Power will be shifted to capital and labor's share of national income will decrease.

The focus of Pastor and Dymski's analysis is the private sector, but wage suppression has also occurred in the public sector as part of many expenditure reduction programs (Feinberg). In an effort to decrease aggregate demand and restore fiscal balance, the wages of public sector employees are often allowed to decrease in real terms. As a result of the downward pressure on wages in both the private and public sectors, poverty will tend to increase among workers in these sectors. Despite the fact that most of the employment in these sectors is in urban areas, because rural and urban labor markets are linked by migration, even rural workers not directly affected by the industrial or public sector labor market will suffer a downward pressure on their wages. Rural wages will also suffer because income generated from the sale of agricultural goods in the domestic market will tend to decline *ceteris paribus* as the fall in per capita income decreases the demand for agricultural products.

In addition to the negative effects on long run growth and short run wage and employment levels, reductions in public expenditure may also have an important impact on the welfare of the poor if cuts in social sector spending are included. In many LDCs the public sector provides the only access to education and health care for low income households, and public subsidies for food and basic needs have an important impact on the household budget. Although there is much debate about the efficiency of such spending in improving welfare indicators like infant mortality and nutritional status, it is extremely likely that the removal of these programs would decrease the welfare of the poor.

While it is relatively easy to identify the probable welfare effects of decreases in social spending, it is less easy to predict how social spending will fare during an adjustment program. Spending on education seems to have decreased as a fraction of GDP in most adjusting nations (Morley, Cornia), but there is some disagreement as to whether spending on health has fallen, or merely stopped growing and held roughly constant in real terms (Grooteart, Morley, Cornia). There are even some important examples, like Mexico, where social spending actually increased during part of the adjustment process. The overall conclusion of a study by Hicks and Kubisch (cited in Streeten, 1989b), which examined a large number of adjusting countries, is that while there have been drastic cuts in some countries and modest increases in others, on average, social expenditures have fallen but been cut less than other types of public expenditure.

The Effects of Expenditure Switching

Expenditure switching policies are designed to reallocate resources to the production of tradables in order to improve the balance of trade by increasing the level of domestic production of tradables for a given level of aggregate demand, and also in order to increase growth by improving efficiency (Bourguignon *et al.*, 1991b). Although there may be some short run contractionary effects associated with switching policies, the higher growth rate, if in fact the policies are successful in stimulating higher growth, is unlikely to harm anyone. However, the shifting resources from one sector of the economy to another may have a significant impact on the employment and income of the poor, depending on where the poor are employed. For example, in economies in which most traded goods are agricultural goods and the poor are employed primarily in the agricultural sector, the poor will tend to benefit from the shift of resources (Streeten, 1989b). However, in most LDCs, low income workers are distributed across various sectors and such reallocations will tend to benefit some while impoverishing others. The strength of this differential effect will ultimately depend on the mobility of labor between sectors.

The most important tool for achieving expenditure switching in most adjustment programs is a real devaluation of the currency. A devaluation may affect the welfare of the poor not only through altering the composition of production, but also by increasing the cost of imported consumer goods and by increasing inflation (Feinburg, Morley). While in many LDCs imported consumer goods are primarily luxury goods, in others, basic foodstuffs, which are part of the consumption bundle of the poor, are important. In these cases, the real purchasing power of the poor will be hurt by devaluation.

Inflation may affect poverty through two main channels (Morley). The first is the effect of inflation on the value of financial assets. The poor tend to hold their money in cash instead of the domestic-indexed or foreign-denominated financial instruments which are commonly used by high income groups. The value of the cash balances of the poor will erode during high inflation and the difference in return between the financial assets of the poor and non-poor will tend to worsen inequality. The second channel through which inflation may affect poverty is the changes in the real wage which may be associated with accelerating inflation. Because of a lack of bargaining power, full indexation of wages is less common among the poor (Lustig, 1995). Thus, although there may not be a strong relation between the inflation rate and real wages when inflation is stable and workers have time to adjust their behavior and expectations, during periods of accelerating inflation, nominal wages are unlikely to keep pace with price increases and the real wages of the poor will fall.

The Effects of Institutional and Policy Reform

The institutional and policy reforms included in most adjustment programs are designed to move the economy towards greater openness and market-orientation, with less government intervention. The policy changes typically include trade reform, the removal of price subsidies and controls, financial liberalization, and privatization.

There are two principal reasons why these policy changes may be expected to affect poverty. The first is that reforms are expected to change the composition of output and improve the growth rate of the economy. The second is that the nature of state intervention will be changed and its scope reduced.

The Effects of Liberalization on Poverty

It is widely argued that the removal of trade barriers associated with imort substitution industrialization (ISI) will have a positive impact on poverty and income distribution (Goldin, 1990). There are three reasons to expect that liberalization will tend to reduce poverty and income inequality. The first is that the removal of trade policies which were designed to decrease the cost of importing capital goods should make production more labor intensive (Khan, 1993). More labor intensive production, coupled with faster growth, should increase wage income. According to the Heckscher-Ohlin and Stolper-Samuelson theorems, a move towards freer trade will tend to increase real wages in nations with an abundant supply of labor (Alarcon). Because labor is generally the most important factor of production for the poor, and is relatively equally distributed, the trade liberalization should result in less poverty and greater equality.

These potential benefits of greater openness depend on the extent to which the economy is able to respond to changes in relative prices. The realization of the potential depends on how quickly and completely the economy is able to reallocate resources and change the composition of production to take advantage of the changed incentives (Griffin). The likelihood of the benefits of improved long run growth outweighing the costs of restructuring are greatest in economies in which there is new investment in newly profitable sectors of the economy, as opposed to a static reallocation of resources (Griffin).

The second reason to expect liberalization to have a positive effect on poverty and income distribution is that there are likely to be large costs associated with the distortion of relative prices caused by protectionist policies (Rosegrant). By reducing these distortions, liberalization should promote a more efficient allocation of resources. In addition to the static gains from improved resource allocation, liberalization may also improve productivity by allowing producers access to less expensive and higher quality intermediate goods and allowing them to take advantage of the economies of scale provided by the size of the international market (Dornsbusch). This greater efficiency should then stimulate more rapid growth throughout the economy. Though there is no reason to expect it to reduce inequality, higher growth should help to reduce poverty by generating employment and wage income.

Whether these reforms actually achieve the expected results is a subject of extensive debate in the literature. In an extensive review article Edwards (1993) points out that many of the cross country empirical studies which purported to demonstrate a relationship between liberalization and growth were focused on the degree of anti-export bias and not government intervention. As such, those countries in which import restrictions were accompanied by heavy export subsidies were treated as liberalized despite extensive government involvement in the economy (Pastor and Conroy). While the developments in endogenous growth theory make a more convincing case for the relationship between long run growth and trade policy, attempts to analyze these models empirically have suffered from the same difficulties in measuring trade orientation as the earlier cross country studies (Edwards).

The third reason to expect liberalization to affect poverty is that in import substituting economies, agriculture is frequently disadvantaged by policies which reallocate resources to the urban manufacturing and service sectors; for example, overvalued exchange rates weaken the competitiveness of agricultural commodities in international markets and tariff and non-tariff barriers increase input costs (Goldin and Winters). In most LDCs poverty rates are higher in rural areas, and it is agriculture which provides the basis for employment and income for the majority of the poor. Thus, policies which discriminate against agriculture will tend to exacerbate poverty and inequality. A shift in trade policy towards a more liberal trade regime will remove some of these market distortions and change the internal terms of trade in favor of agriculture. The improvement in the internal terms of trade of agriculture should stimulate faster growth in the agricultural sector, which will tend to decrease poverty and improve the distribution of income.

Sectoral Policy

The arguments that liberalization will have a positive effect on poverty and income distribution focus on the likely economywide effects of the reforms; however, they often ignore the likely effects of changes in sectoral policy. In the case of certain sectors this can be a critical oversight. For example, there is heavy state intervention in the agricultural sector of most LDCs. This means that liberalization of their agricultural sectors will mean moving toward more market-oriented policies not only in international, but also domestic markets. This is important for poverty and income distribution because the state interventions in agricultural markets frequently have specific income objectives. As such, their elimination is likely to have strong income effects. In cases where the benefits of state intervention are captured primarily by relatively prosperous farmers, the distributional impact may be positive. In cases where state interventions are designed to support the incomes of relatively poor producers of less competitive crops, the effect of liberalization on poverty and income distribution is likely to be negative.

Empirical Approaches

Model-Based Simulations

The model-based counterfactual analyses compare the results of adjustment programs with the results of simulations of alternative policies. The simulations are designed to give some indication if alternative sets of policies would have had lower social costs. The conclusion of an OECD study which included simulations for a group of six diverse economies[1] is that the social costs of adjustment could have been somewhat lower, but that because the adjustment programs included measures designed to mitigate the negative effects on vulnerable groups, alternative policies would not have achieved a large decrease in social costs (Bourgiognon *et al.*, 1991b).

The studies also highlight the difficulty of generalizing about the likely effects of adjustment on poverty; because institutional characteristics, market adjustment mechanisms and initial conditions vary greatly across economies, an identical set of adjustment policies may have very different distributional effects for different economies (Bourguignon *et al.*, 1991b). Despite this caution against generalizing, the OECD studies did generate one important result which was consistent across all six studies: when the hypothetical counterfactual is specified as "no policy change", that is, import rationing is allowed to satisfy the external constraint, the results of the simulations suggest that the social costs of doing nothing would have been much higher than those suffered under the adjustment programs (Morrisson, 1991).

The studies analyzed various sets of policy alternatives, with most simulating the effect of alternative policies for decreasing the fiscal deficit and devaluing the currency. The results for the simulations of devaluation policies were mixed. The simulation exercises for the six different economies suggest that the choice of this policy tool was generally favorable for the poor in the short run, but that when the long run effects were taken into account, the results were varied (Bourguignon *et al.*, 1991b). In the short run, a devaluation was preferable to a reduction in public spending because it stimulates exports and avoids the contractionary impact of a decrease in spending. However, because a devaluation will tend to stimulate inflation and drive up interest rates, the long run effects on growth and poverty were less desirable. In the simulations for Ecuador and Morocco, the increases in inflation and interest rates lowered investment. The lower investment decreased long run growth enough to make alternative policies more attractive for their effect on income distribution and poverty (de Janvry *et al.*; Morrisson, 1991). In Indonesia, inflation also increased in the long run, but growth was not affected; however, the devaluation does produce a disequalizing shift in the income distribution, exacerbating poverty (Thorbecke). In contrast, the simulation for Côte d'Ivoire generated a decrease in poverty in the long run due to the employment increase associated with higher export growth (Lambert *et al.*).

The simulations of the alternative policies for decreasing the fiscal deficit included examinations of tax increases, real wage reductions, and cuts in current and capital expenditures. In Côte d'Ivoire and Morocco the primary means of closing the fiscal gap was the reduction of public sector wages and slowing the growth in public employment. The simulations for both Côte d'Ivoire and Morocco indicated that the wage cut was the only alternative to have positive distributional effects; the equalizing effect results from the fact that most state workers are in the middle or upper reaches of the income distribution (Bourguignon *et al.*, 1991b). In the case of Morocco, the alternative with the worst effect on poverty was the elimination of state sector jobs, and the alternative with the best effect on poverty was the reduction in state expenditure (Bourguignon *et al.*, 1991b).

Country Studies

It is difficult to reach a general conclusion as to how the poverty rate changed in countries undergoing adjustment. In addition to the methodological difficulties mentioned above, there are severe data limitations for most countries. Reliable household level income and expenditure data for the periods just before and after adjustment are not available for most LDCs (Lustig, 1995; Bourguignon *et al.*, 1991b). Nonetheless, the available data do allow the identification of some general trends.

In a wide-ranging review of data from various Latin American countries, Morley (1995) found that the incidence of poverty increased for most adjusting countries. Only in Chile, Costa Rica and Colombia did both urban and rural poverty decline during the 1980s, the period of crisis and adjustment which Morley chose to cover.

In a separate study, Fiszbein and Psacharopoulos (1995) found that changes in income distribution were more varied for Latin American countries undergoing adjustment. Argentina, Brazil, and Paraguay experienced large increases in income inequality, while Costa Rica and Venezuela showed little appreciable change, and Uruguay and Colombia achieved large improvements in income distribution.

In results which differ markedly from those for Latin America, Demery and Squire (1996) report that poverty rates decreased for five of the six African countries undergoing adjustment in their sample. According to Demery and Squire, Côte d'Ivoire, the only country for which poverty rates increased during the period of study, was unable to carry out an adjustment program which included a real devaluation and trade liberalization. The conclusion of Demery and Squire is that it was the relatively successful adjustment programs of the other countries which allowed them to decrease poverty.

Adjusting and Non-adjusting Countries

In a cross-country analysis which does not directly address the issue of poverty, but rather focuses of the relationship between per capita income growth and adjustment policies, Kakwani (1995) presents some evidence to suggest that adjustment policies have a positive impact on poverty. Kakwani divides 77 countries into Intense Adjustment Lending (IAL) countries, Other Adjustment Lending (OAL) countries, and Non-Adjustment Lending (NAL) countries, and examines their growth performance before and after the period when most countries adjusted. He finds that among IAL countries, 59.3 per cent suffered a decrease in per capita income from 1976-80 to 1981-85, the period immediately preceding adjustment, but only 37 per cent suffered a decline from 1981-85 to 1986-90, the period of most intense adjustment. In contrast, in OAL and NAL countries, the percentage suffering a decrease in per capita income for these same periods increased from 36.7 per cent and 45.0 per cent to 66.7 per cent and 60.0 per cent respectively.

Kakwani is careful not to conclude from these data that the superior performance of the IAL countries is due to the adjustment policies. Rather, he constructs a model to test the hypothesis that intensely adjusting countries have experienced superior growth in per capita income when external shocks and initial conditions are controlled for. The results of his regression support this hypothesis: when external shocks and initial conditions are controlled for, intense adjustment appears to be the best policy for promoting growth for the countries in his sample. However, this does not imply that a less intensive adjustment process may not be successful in other contexts. China, for example, was successful in promoting rapid growth through a more gradual adjustment. Nor does it imply that intense adjustment will be the best policy for decreasing poverty. There is no reason to assume that these policies will be distribution neutral. The negative effect of increases in income inequality could outweigh the positive effect of gains in per capita income.

In a different approach to the comparison of adjusting and non-adjusting countries, Demery and Squire (*op. cit.*) use Côte d'Ivoire, a country whose liberalization was unsuccessful and which was unable to devalue its currency because of membership in the CFA franc zone, and Ghana, which was successful in implementing expenditure switching devaluation and trade liberalization, as "counterfactual examples" for each other. They found that the internal adjustment which Côte d'Ivoire underwent had significant social costs. The government was forced to make deep cuts in public expenditure and poverty increased by 15.9 per cent. In contrast, Ghana's successful expenditure switching policies succeeded in restoring growth, and the poverty rate was reduced by 5.5 per cent. Demery and Squire point out that the complex political economy of Côte d'Ivoire may not have permitted the type of adjustment which Ghana implemented, but they reason that if such policies had been implemented in Côte d'Ivoire the poor would have fared much better.

Conclusions

In general, the effects of an adjustment program will be very difficult to predict. There are theoretical reasons to expect that the effects of the primary reforms included in most adjustment packages, *viz.*, fiscal reform, policies to encourage expenditure switching, and institutional and policy reform, may have positive or negative effects on poverty, and that these effects may be different at different stages of adjustment. The net effect will depend on the precise mix of policies followed to achieve the reforms, their timing, the success of their implementation, and the institutional characteristics and initial conditions of the economy in question. Economic theory does not provide a simple, generalizable relationship between adjustment and poverty. Nor do the empirical studies of countries which have already undergone adjustment. There is a great variety of experience in adjusting countries, and empirical studies which have tried to establish a general relationship between poverty and adjustment have differed in their conclusions - some suggest a positive correlation between adjustment programs and improvements in poverty, while others suggest a positive correlation between adjustment and increases in poverty.

Note

[1]   The study included Chile, Côte d'Ivoire, Ecuador, Malaysia, Morocco, and Indonesia.

3 The Adjustment Process in Mexico

This chapter examines the development strategy which was followed in Mexico before adjustment and the policy changes and performance of the economy during the adjustment period. The chapter begins with a review of the strategy of ISI and the events which precipitated the 1982 debt crisis. It then provides a description of the content of the various stabilization and structural adjustment policies which were implemented and of the policies' effects on the economy's performance.

Import Substitution Industrialization

For most of the period from the early 1950s through 1985, the development of the Mexican economy was based on a strategy of import substitution. The protection of Mexican industry included three primary controls: import tariffs, official reference prices, and import licensing restrictions. Of these controls, import licenses were the most important. The extent of the protection varied considerably over time in response to balance of payments shifts, but the basic commitment to protecting domestic industry was maintained until the mid-1980s.[1] The protected environment, combined with generally sound fiscal management and the fortuitous absence of external shocks, allowed the Mexican economy to achieve excellent performance from 1950 through the early 1970s. From 1950 to 1973, output growth averaged six per cent a year and annual inflation rates averaged below three per cent a year.

Growth began to slow in the early 1970s due to the effects of the first oil price shock,[2] the resulting world recession, and a slowdown in productivity growth. The response of the Echeverria administration (1970-1976) to the economic slowdown was to increase public expenditure and the level of state intervention in the economy.[3] The economy responded quickly with the growth rate climbing above six per cent for the 1973 to 1976 period. However, the resumption of rapid growth was gained at the expense of an increase in the fiscal deficit and higher inflation. The surge in public spending was not accompanied by a corresponding increase in revenues, and the fiscal deficit grew from 1.8 per cent of GDP in 1971 to 7.6 per cent of GDP in 1976, and was financed primarily through external borrowing (Belausteguigoita). The rapid growth and fiscal imbalance caused inflation to accelerate. This caused large scale capital flight as domestic investors began to fear a devaluation of the exchange rate. The macroeconomic imbalances reached a point of crisis in 1976 when the Banco de Mexico no longer had sufficient reserves to maintain the fixed exchange rate and the peso was allowed to float for the first time in twenty two years. A sharp devaluation followed, and output fell and inflation increased rapidly.

It is possible that this crisis could have forced a correction of the macroeconomic imbalances, but before large scale reforms could be enacted, the fiscal and foreign exchange constraints were relieved by the discovery of large new oil reserves. The Portillo administration (1976-1982) switched to a strategy of petroleum-led growth, and public expenditure increased sharply to finance the investment necessary to exploit the petroleum reserves. In response to the increase in public spending and surge in private investment, the economy began to grow rapidly. From 1978 to 1981, growth averaged over eight per cent a year, and per capita income approached the levels of industrialized economies like Greece and Portugal (Ten Kate, 1992b).

The Portillo administration believed that the oil boom would result in a permanent increase in the nation's income and increased public expenditure accordingly; but by 1982, a series of external and internal factors combined to end the petroleum based boom in a new foreign exchange crisis. The increase in aggregate demand associated with this rapid growth generated upward pressure on the prices of non-tradable goods, and the resulting inflation led to an overvalued exchange rate (Lustig, 1995). This made it difficult for other sectors of the economy to compete in the international market, and exports became increasingly dominated by the petroleum sector. The value of manufacturing exports actually fell by five per cent from 1980 to 1982, and by late 1981, petroleum products accounted for 70 per cent of Mexico's export earnings (Lustig and Ros). At the same time, the increase in aggregate demand and the overvalued exchange rate caused a surge in imports. By 1982, despite the large increase in oil exports, the balance of trade had actually worsened.

In addition to the deteriorating balance of trade, the size of the fiscal deficit was growing rapidly. The increase in public spending, which was undertaken in anticipation of future oil revenues, caused the fiscal deficit to increase to 9.8 per cent of GDP in 1981 (Dornbusch and Werner). This gap was financed by external borrowing. At the time, both the Mexican government and the international financial institutions believed that oil prices would continue to rise and that credit would continue to be available at low interest rates.[4] Both these beliefs proved wrong, and the result of their mistaken predictions proved disastrous.

In mid-1981 international oil prices began to fall. Mexico refused to lower its price at first and lost market share before finally being forced to drop its price. At the same time, international interest rates began to climb and there was large scale capital flight as investors began to fear another devaluation. Mexico thus entered 1982 in an untenable situation, *viz.*, with a very large and growing foreign debt, the prospect of sustained high interest rates which would fuel the growth of the debt in the medium term, and an overvalued exchange rate and inward looking economy which made it impossible to generate the foreign exchange necessary to service the debt. The Portillo administration was forced to suspend payment on the external debt in August of 1982 and a severe crisis followed. The annual inflation rate soared to nearly 100 per cent and the economy shrank by 0.5 per cent for the year (Tables 3.1 and 3.2).

Adjustment Policies and Economic Performance

In December of 1982, the de la Madrid administration (1982-1988) instituted an orthodox stabilization program. The program was designed to restore price stability and improve the ability to service the external debt through fiscal adjustment and a devaluation of the currency, but it did not include major structural reform. In order to generate the resources necessary to service the debt, the currency was devalued sharply and the primary fiscal deficit, which had been 8.5 per cent of GDP in 1981, was converted into a 4.2 per cent surplus by 1983 (Lustig, 1992). In order to generate the fiscal surplus, non-interest government spending had to be cut sharply. The greatest reductions were in public investment, particularly in rural development, fishing, and tourism.

The stabilization program initially succeeded in reducing inflation from its peak of nearly 100 per cent in 1983 to 60 per cent in 1984. The program also succeeded in generating a current account surplus for 1983. However, the deep cuts in public expenditure caused the economy to shrink by over four per cent in 1983. The severity of the recession caused the government to relax its contractionary policies. The economy responded with a mild recovery in 1984 and early 1985, but the increase in imports associated with this increased growth and the appreciating peso, coupled with falling oil prices, caused a rapid deterioration in the balance of trade. At the same time, inflation began to accelerate due to the program's lack of credibility and some inertia in the wage-price dynamic.

These balance of trade problems and accelerating inflation forced the adoption of a new stabilization program in July of 1985. Unlike the previous stabilization program, the contractionary fiscal and monetary policies of the 1985 program were accompanied by a rapid acceleration of trade liberalization.[5] At this time, policy makers were becoming convinced that the lack of growth was due to the inefficient production structures resulting from protectionist policies, counterproductive government intervention in the economy, and an "irrational" resistance to foreign investment (Ten Kate, 1992b). It was believed that to stimulate growth, the root causes of economic stagnation needed to be addressed. This implied liberalizing trade, privatizing government enterprises, and opening the economy to foreign investment.

The trade reforms of 1985 eliminated quantitative controls on almost all intermediate goods and many capital goods. The focus was initially on decreasing import licensing requirements, which were the most important barrier to trade. The share of imports covered by import licenses was cut from 92 per cent in June to 47 per cent in December of 1985 (Table 3.3). In order to compensate for this loss of protection, tariffs and official reference prices were increased temporarily, but in 1987 tariff rates were cut sharply, and by 1988 all official reference prices had been eliminated (Table 3.3).

In order to improve the balance of trade and mitigate the impact of liberalization on import-competitors, the real exchange rate was steadily devalued from July of 1985 through 1986 (Chart 3.1). The devaluation of the peso was successful in stimulating exports, and Mexico began to accumulate large stocks of foreign reserves. The devaluation also succeeded in greatly improving the competitiveness of non-oil exports - the share of non-oil export in total exports increased from 32 per cent in 1985 to 61 per cent in 1986 (Table 3.1). These conditions favored further liberalization, and Mexico reversed its increase in tariff and official price protection and acceded to GATT in 1986. However, the continued depreciation of the peso meant that domestic prices were not anchored by the exchange rate (Ten Kate, 1992b). This added inflationary pressure to the wage-price dynamic, and when a speculative attack on the peso followed the October 1987 stock market collapse, it became apparent that, despite a commitment to liberalization, there was a dangerous volatility in expectations (Lustig, 1992). If the economy was to recover its high growth rates, inflation had to be brought under control.

In order to control its persistent inflation, Mexico moved away from conventional aggregate demand adjustment programs and instituted a heterodox adjustment program in 1987. In addition to the orthodox policies of further fiscal and monetary restraint, the 1987 program included three additional components: an incomes policy designed to break the inertia of inflation, acceleration of liberalization designed to speed structural reform, and a fixed nominal exchange rate designed to provide an anchor for prices. After 1987, the exchange rate policy was shifted to a crawling peg until it was allowed to float during the peso crisis of 1994.

The heterodox reform was based on the premise that inflation had a strong inertial component (Aspe). This implies that even if the economic imbalances were corrected, inflation would tend to continue at a high rate, and the demand restraint policies designed to correct the imbalances would tend to cause a deep recession (Agénor). The key to the heterodox program's potential for success was the incomes policy. Through a process of *concertación*, or negotiation among representatives of government, industry, labor, and agricultural producers, the government was able to secure a commitment from industry not to raise prices and from labor not to push for real wage increases. The Economic Solidarity Pact formalized these agreements, and careful monitoring and frequent adjustments prevented rigidities from forming.

The results of the 1987 adjustment were striking. The monthly inflation rate fell from fifteen per cent in January to one per cent in December of 1988; the annual rate fell from 140 per cent in 1988 to 20 per cent in 1989 and stayed at roughly this level until 1993 when it fell to single digits. Real income growth was slowed in 1988, but recovered quickly and averaged 3.7 per cent a year from 1989 to 1992. Inflation had finally been brought under control and at a relatively small cost in terms of lost output. In addition, by the late 1980s, fiscal and monetary balance had been achieved, and the transition to a more open economy was essentially complete.

The long adjustment process necessary to bring the Mexican economy to this point was very costly. From 1982 to 1987 the average annual growth in GDP was roughly zero per cent, and GDP per capita fell by ten per cent; the growth in GDP per capita was roughly nine per cent from

1988 to 1994, but despite the renewed growth, the GDP per capita in 1994 was still two per cent lower than in 1981 (Table 3.3).   In addition, investment and expenditure on social programs had been reduced sharply. There was an urgent need for renewed growth, but the resumption of the high rates of growth necessary to regain the standard of living enjoyed before the crisis was far from assured.

The return of sustainable higher growth was limited by the large net transfers of resources abroad. The interest payments on the enormous external debt, large scale capital flight, and the reduction of foreign investment and external credit meant that the flow of net transfers from Mexico was equal to six per cent of GDP from 1983 to 1988 (Aspe). The low rate of investment during the adjustment period made it particularly important for Mexico to reverse this lose of resources.

In order to reduce the net transfers abroad, the Salinas administration (1988-1994) sought to re-negotiate the principal and service of its foreign debt. In mid-1989 it signed the Brady Plan, an agreement with foreign creditors which decreased its medium and long term debt from 76 per cent of GDP to 30 per cent of GDP (Aspe). The agreement reversed the net transfer of resources and was perceived as an important positive signal to potential investors. In order to further stimulate investment and reverse capital flight, the Salinas administration also accelerated the changes being made in Mexico's development strategy.   In addition to liberalization, new reforms sought to decrease state intervention and regulation in the economy. A wave of highly significant privatizations were undertaken, including the national telecommunications company and the commercial banks which had been nationalized under the de la Madrid administration, with the aim of increasing business confidence and increasing efficiency.[6]   An additional important step taken to boost investor confidence was Salinas' 1990 announcement that Mexico would pursue a free trade agreement with the United States and Canada. The North American Free Trade Agreement, which eventually came into effect in 1994, was seen by investors not only as an opportunity for new investment, but also as a sign of Mexico's commitment to its more liberal trade policies and development strategy.

The combination of debt renegotiation, renewed investor confidence in Mexico, and low interest rates in the United States stimulated large flows of capital into Mexico. Net capital inflows, which had been negative from 1982 to 1988, were a positive $3 billion in 1989 and reached $30 billion in 1993 (Dornbusch and Werner; Levy). By 1994, what was seen by the Salinas administration as the primary obstacle to renewed growth, the net transfer of resources abroad, had been reversed; inflation had fallen to single digits; and GDP growth had rebounded, averaging approximately three per cent a year from 1989 through 1994. It appeared that the Mexican economy was finally poised to enter a new period of sustainable long term growth.

Beginning in 1992, however, a very large current account deficit began to emerge. The nominal exchange rate was initially fixed in the 1987 stabilization and then allowed to follow a crawling peg. The exchange rate policy, though initially effective as an anchor for nominal prices, caused the real exchange rate to appreciate steadily as domestic inflation remained above the level of Mexico's main trading partners. The overvalued exchange rate damaged the international competitiveness of Mexican industry and helped to fuel an import boom, nearly a third of which consisted of consumer goods and intermediate goods destined for re-export. The resulting current account deficit was financed primarily by the large capital inflows.

Mexican policy makers challenged the notion that the peso was overvalued. They pointed out that the equilibrium exchange rate is difficult to calculate and that the sharp devaluation of the currency before the reform had probably left the peso undervalued; therefore, the subsequent nominal appreciation did not necessarily mean that the peso was overvalued (Ortiz). They argued that an appreciation was the natural consequence of borrowing in order to invest in productive capital. Critics of the exchange rate policy pointed out that the financial flows which were financing the external deficit were fragile and that much of the inflow of foreign funds went to support consumption and the import of intermediate goods (Dornbusch and Werner). The critics called for a real depreciation, not appreciation, to accompany the liberalization of trade in order to stimulate demand for domestic production.

The surge in capital inflows was a function of both external and internal factors. Among the most important external factors were the reduction in short term international interest rates, the recession in industrialized countries; and changes in US capital market regulations which reduced the transactions costs for Mexican issuers (Gurría). The most important internal factors were the increased investor confidence which the reforms generated and high domestic interest rates which began as a part of the stabilization policies and were continued as part of a policy of partial sterilization of capital inflows (Gurría). However, the receipt of such large capital inflows created the risk that aggregate demand would expand too quickly and increase inflationary pressure. In order to neutralize this risk, the Mexican government employed a range of measures to absorb the flow. These measures included increasing the band in which the peso was allowed to fluctuate as increasing foreign capital flows put pressure on the currency; privatizing state firms to help absorb excess liquidity; and limiting banks' foreign currency liabilities (Gurría).

In 1994, a series of political shocks in Mexico caused international investors to become concerned about the currency risk of Mexican investments. These fears, combined with higher interest rates in the United States, caused capital flows to slow from $30 billion in 1993 to just $10 billion in 1994. During 1994 two major runs on the peso also occurred. Election year politics made the conventional response to speculative attacks, *viz.*, an increase in interest rates and a weakening of the currency, unattractive. The contractionary fiscal and monetary policy which could have closed the current account deficit was also unattractive in the run up to the election. Policies to correct the current account imbalance were not undertaken, and the government was forced to finance the deficit primarily through a reduction of foreign exchange reserves which fell from $30 billion in January of 1994 to $5 billion on December 22, 1994 (Levy).

When the foreign exchange reserves became critically low, the Zedillo administration was forced to attempt a fifteen per cent devaluation of the peso. The devaluation surprised the international financial community and generated panic among institutional investors.[7] There was a massive redemption of short term government debt, the private sector lost access to international capital markets, and the government was forced to allow the peso to float. Once allowed to float, the sudden drop in demand for Mexican financial instruments caused the value of the peso to plummet.

In March of 1995, the Zedillo administration announced a new stabilization program designed to control the inflationary pressure generated by the enormous devaluation and to rebuild international confidence in the economy. The program included the adoption of a floating exchange rate with monetary policy designed to stabilize prices, an intensive supervision and regulation of the banking industry program designed to prevent widespread bankruptcies, and a fiscal contraction designed to increase the primary surplus to 4.4 per cent; however, the program also increased real expenditure for social sector and rural programs by two per cent. The devaluation and adjustment programs caused a severe recession in 1995 with the economy shrinking by nearly seven per cent. A moderate recovery occurred relatively quickly, and GDP growth exceeded five per cent in 1996; inflation rose to 35 per cent in 1995 and stayed at roughly the same level for 1996 (INEGI, 1997).

Summary

From 1982 until the close of the decade, the Mexican economy underwent a series of profound changes. In order to reduce inflation and move toward greater efficiency, chronic fiscal imbalances were corrected, external trade was liberalized, markets were deregulated, and ownership regulations were changed to make investment in the economy more attractive. By the end of the decade these reforms has been successful in bringing inflation under control, generating moderate GDP growth, reversing the net transfer of resources abroad, and transforming the incentives governing production. These changes were achieved at extremely high costs in terms of foregone growth, reduced investment, cuts in social services, and political turmoil, and thus raise important questions about how the poor faired during adjustment.

In addition, the sustainabability of the recovery and the strategies followed in the late 1980s and early 1990s were brought into question by the peso crisis of December 1994. The exchange rate policy which had been one of the keys to controlling inflation, also helped to generate a large current account deficit which made Mexico very dependent on foreign capital inflows. The peso crisis demonstrated the danger of Mexico's reliance on foreign capital inflows, particularly highly liquid portfolio investments, as nervous international investors quickly withdrew funds from the Mexican economy, greatly exacerbating the effects of a mishandled devaluation.

Table 3.1: Indicators of Economic Performance, 1981-1994 (percent changes)

	Inflation (CPI)	Inflation (Dec/Dec)	Imports	Exports	Non-oil Exports	B.O.T.
1981	27.9	28.7	17.7	11.6	9.0	-3.8
1982	58.9	98.8	-37.9	21.8	-14.0	6.8
1983	101.9	80.8	-33.8	13.6	32.5	13.8
1984	65.4	59.2	17.8	5.7	20.7	12.9
1985	57.7	63.7	11.0	4.5	-9.2	7.1
1986	86.2	105.7	-12.4	3.2	41.0	3.7
1987	131.8	159.2	5.0	10.1	23.7	7.2
1988	114.2	51.7	36.7	5.8	15.2	0.3
1989	20.0	19.7	21.3	2.5	7.5	-2.6
1990	26.7	29.9	18.8	3.5	12.0	-4.4
1991	22.7	18.8	16.6	5.1	12.8	-11.3
1992	15.5	11.9	24.3	8.2	9.7	-20.7
1993	9.8	8.0	5.2	12.3	17.4	-19.1
1994	7.0	--	21.4	17.2	--	--

Source: La Economia Mexicana en Cifras, various years.

Table 3.2:   Real GDP and Real GDP per capita, 1981-1994

	GDP	GDP (percent change)	GDP per capita	GDP per capita (percent change)
1981	4,862	8.8	7,087	5.9
1982	4,831	-0.6	6,881	-3.1
1983	4,269	-4.2	6,447	-6.5
1984	4.796	3.6	6,542	1.2
1985	4,920	0.3	6,577	0.3
1986	4,735	-5.9	6,213	-5.9
1987	4,823	-0.3	6,215	-0.3
1988	4,883	1.2	6,188	-0.8
1989	5,047	3.3	6,285	1.3
1990	5,272	4.4	6,452	2.5
1991	5,463	3.6	6,558	1.7
1992	5,616	2.8	6,607	1.1
1993	5,659	0.4	6,527	-1.3
1994	5,858	3.6	6,748	1.4

Note: GDP figures are millions of 1980 pesos.   GDP per capita figures are 1980 pesos.
Source: La Economia Mexicana en Cifras (1995), World Bank Data Tables (1994).

Table 3.3: Aggregate Indicators of Trade Liberalization

	ILC[a]	ORP[b]	AT[c]	MS[d]
1985 (June)	92.2	18.7	23.5	9.3
1985 (Dec.)	47.1	35.4	28.5	9.3
1986 (June)	46.9	19.6	24.0	9.0
1986 (Dec.)	39.8	18.7	24.5	9.0
1987 (June)	35.8	13.4	22.7	9.3
1987 (Dec.)	25.4	0.6	11.8	9.3
1988	21.3	0.0	10.2	13.1
1989	19.8	0.0	12.5	14.6
1990	7.9	0.0	12.4	--

Note: [a] Import license coverage as proportion of domestic production.
[b] Official reference price coverage as proportion of domestic production.
[c] Average nominal tariff.
[d] Import share in internal demand for manufacturing at constant prices.

Source: Weiss (1992) and Alarcon (1992).

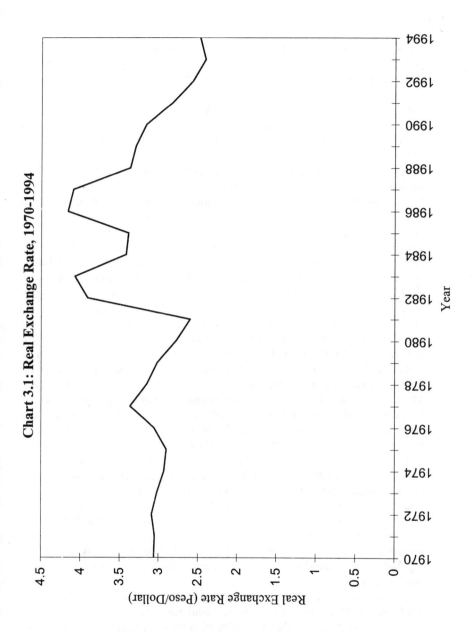

Chart 3.1: Real Exchange Rate, 1970-1994

Notes

1   Despite this commitment to protection, the Mexican economy was far from closed. Estimates for the period of ISI by Weiss (1992) show that the net effect of the trade controls was less protectionist in Mexico than in many countries.

2   Mexico was still a net importer of oil at this time.

3   Lustig (1992) points out that the increase in public spending and intervention in the economy was only partially in response to slower economic growth. The Echeverria administration directed much of the spending towards the social sector in response to the high level of social tension which had continued since the student riots of 1968.

4   In 1979 Mexico was receiving approximately $20 per barrel for its crude oil. The 1980 *World Development Report* forecast that real oil prices would increase to over $35 a barrel in 1985 and over $40 a barrel in 1990. The 1981 *World Development Report* increased these estimates, predicting that the real price per barrel would exceed $42 by 1990. Had oil prices stabilized at the expected level, the earnings from Mexico's oil exports would very likely have been sufficient to service the level of foreign debt it had incurred by 1982, and the debt crisis could have been avoided (Lustig, 1992).

5   While the turning point in Mexican trade policies is usually identified as mid-1985, significant changes toward greater openness in the economy had begun as early as the 1970s. Import restrictions were relaxed in the late 1970s as the foreign exchange constraint was loosened by the increase in oil exports and Mexico began to prepare for entry into GATT. At the turn of the decade, Mexico had a relatively liberal trade regime compared to previous decades. In 1980, the decision to postpone entry into GATT and the building debt crisis reversed the trend. Despite the professed desire to move towards a more open economy, the Portillo administration reacted to the 1982 debt crisis by increasing protection; in particular, the coverage of import licenses was sharply increased. The de la Madrid administration began some tentative moves toward liberalization in 1983, but by June of 1985, 92 per cent of imports required licenses, up from just 64 per cent in 1980 (Weiss).

6   The number of public enterprises decreased from over 1,100 in 1982 to 257 by 1992 (Lustig and Ros; Aspe, 1992). Although many of these privatizations occurred before the Salinas administration took office, the number of privatizations involving important high profile firms was much greater under Salinas.

7   Calvo and Mendoza (1996) argue that the sudden withdrawal of investment funds had little to do with economic fundamentals. They show that the extremely high cost of gathering information on a large number of economies implies that portfolio allocations to a single country are highly responsive to small changes in expected returns. For the global investor, the type of herd

behavior displayed in the massive withdrawal of funds from Mexico represents a sensible re-allocation of assets within their portfolio given the high cost of information.

4 Poverty in Mexico During the Period of Adjustment

The adjustment process involves a complex mix of policies whose effect on poverty is very difficult to predict *a priori*. These policies may have differing effects on poverty at different times: expenditure reduction policies will have a contractionary effect on the economy and are likely to have a negative effect on poverty; expenditure switching and policy and institutional reform may ultimately have a positive effect on poverty if the produce more rapid growth, but their effect will depend on the sectors in which the poor are employed, the speed with which they can produce a more efficient structure of production, and the costs associated with the restructuring.

It is clear that the adjustment process, the changes in development strategy, and the exogenous shocks described in the previous chapter had a profound effect on the performance of the Mexican economy. However, it is difficult to anticipate how these changes have the affected the lot of the poor. Most attempts to determine the effect of the adjustment process on the poor have had to infer changes in poverty rates from macroeconomic aggregates - this is an imprecise exercise which does not typically take account of changes in inequality or changes in the performance of different sectors of the economy. Fortunately, detailed household level income and expenditure data exist for Mexico for several years during the adjustment period. These data allow for the measurement of poverty at the household level.

This chapter uses data on household level expenditure to measure how poverty rates changed during the period of adjustment. Both extreme and moderate poverty are estimated, and the extent to which changes in poverty are due to changes in inequality, as opposed to changes in the growth rate, are examined.

The Measurement of Poverty

There is a large theoretical literature on the measurement of poverty.[1] The literature includes discussions on how to quantify the standard of living of a human being and how to determine the minimum acceptable standard of living. Human welfare has many dimensions, *viz.*, health, education, housing, nutrition, which in principle can be measured directly. However, for reasons of data availability, indirect measures of welfare, like income or expenditure per capita, are typically used as the metric for standard of living. The minimum acceptable standard of living, or poverty line, is typically defined according to some notion of the physical and social requirements for life. Individuals who cannot attain the basic physical requirements for life are considered extremely poor, while those who cannot attain the more broadly defined basic needs of life are considered moderately poor. The extreme poverty line is usually defined as the value of the goods necessary to meet basic nutritional requirements, while the moderate poverty line is usually defined as the value of the basket of goods which provides the socially determined basic needs of a particular society. The values of both the minimum nutritional requirements[2] and the goods necessary to fulfill a given society's basic needs are controversial. For this reason, poverty lines with markedly different values are often defined for a single population.

The literature has also established several properties which are generally accepted as desirable in poverty measures. The first of these properties is additive decomposability (Ravallion and Huppi). Additively decomposable measures are those for which aggregate poverty can be represented as weighted sums of poverty levels for subgroups of the population. This property ensures that *ceteris paribus* increases in poverty in one subgroup of the population will cause the poverty measure for the entire population to increase. Poverty measures which are additively decomposable also have the useful attribute that they allow for the analysis of differences in poverty across subgroups of a given population. The second property is satisfaction of the monotonicity axiom (Sen). This property requires that a poverty measure should decrease when the income of the poor increases. The third property requires the satisfaction of the transfer axiom (Sen). Satisfaction of the transfer axiom requires that the poverty measure increases when income is transferred from relatively poor individuals below the poverty line to less poor individuals below the poverty line.

In 1984, Foster, Greer and Thorbecke (FGT) proposed a class of poverty measures which are additively decomposable and some of which meet the requirements of the monotonicity and transfer axioms. The FGT poverty indices can be written generally as:

$$P_\alpha = \left(\frac{1}{n}\right)\sum_{i=1}^{q}\left(\frac{Z-Y_i}{Z}\right)^\alpha$$

Where n is the total population, Z is the poverty line, q is the population whose income (or expenditure) falls below the poverty line, Y_i is the income (or expenditure) of the ith individual, and α is a parameter which can take the values 0,1,2.

When α takes the value of zero, P_α defines the head count index. The head count index is simply the fraction of the population whose income falls short of the poverty line. The headcount index measures the extent of poverty, but does not distinguish between those individuals whose income falls just short of the poverty line and those whose income is far below it.

When α is equal to one, the equation above defines the proportional poverty gap (PPG). The PPG does take account of the level of income of the poor, i.e. the intensity of the poverty, thus meeting the monotonicity axiom. The PPG weights the head count index by the ratio of the average income shortfall of the poor to the poverty line.

When α equals two, the equation above defines the FGT index. The FGT accounts for the severity of poverty by giving greater weight to the income of the poorest individuals. By accounting for the effect of the income inequality among the poor, the FGT satisfies the transfer axiom.

Poverty Estimates for 1984-1994

In order to examine the evolution of poverty over the period of adjustment in Mexico, I have estimated poverty rates for the FGT family of indices using data on per capita household expenditure from the National Household Income Expenditure Survey (ENIGH) for 1984, 1989, 1992, and 1994.[3] The four surveys were administered using a consistent methodology and provide results which are comparable over time.[4]

As was mentioned earlier, in the literature on poverty, the extreme poverty line is defined as the value of the goods necessary to meet basic nutritional requirements, and the moderate poverty line is defined as the value of the goods which provide the basic needs as determined by a particular society. The poverty lines used to calculate extreme and moderate poverty are based on a study of basic needs by the Mexican government agency the *Coordinación General de Plan Nacional de Zonas Deprimidas y Grupos Marginados* (General Coordinator for the National Plan for Marginal Zones, COPLAMAR). The study constructed a basket of goods which met the basic needs of an average household in the seventh income decile. The basket of goods, termed the *Canasta Normativa de Satisfactores Esenciales* (CNSE), included food, housing, clothing, education, health care, culture, transportation and some incidentals. In order to construct the CNSE, COPLAMAR surveyed households in the seventh income decile to determine their consumption patterns. It then estimated the cost of the items it deemed necessary to meet basic needs based on these consumption patterns at market prices.[5]

The study of basic needs also identified a subset of the CNSE, called the *Canasta Normativa Alimentaria* (CNA), which included only the foodstuffs necessary to fulfill basic nutrition requirements. The CNA component of the basic consumption basket includes thirty four different items designed to provide 2,082 calories and 35.1 grams of protein per adult per day.[6]

In order to estimate the rate of extreme poverty, the extreme poverty line is defined as the value of the CNA plus an additional twenty five per cent to account for the "irreducible non-food items" necessary for a household.[7] The value of the extreme poverty line is 66,727 pesos of monthly expenditure per capita in September, 1989 prices; this was equivalent to approximately $25 a month at market exchange rates, which is slightly lower than the dollar a day poverty line employed by the World Bank.[8]

In order to estimate the rate of moderate poverty, the monetary value of the CNSE is defined as the moderate poverty line. The value of the moderate poverty line is 263,003 pesos of monthly expenditure per capita; this was equal to approximately $98 a month at market exchange rates.[9]

Expenditure was chosen as the proxy for well-being for two reasons. The first is that there is likely to be consumption smoothing among the poor during the period of adjustment. Poverty estimates based on household income would not reflect the consumption smoothing behavior. The second is that household income tends to be underreported in income-expenditure surveys. A comprehensive study by Altimir (1982) has shown that income-expenditure surveys in Mexico tend to underestimate income and that the underreporting tends to be of a larger magnitude in higher income groups. The ENIGH appears to follow this general pattern:

Levy (1991) points out that when households are divided in twenty equally sized groups and ordered by income, total expenditure exceeds total income for all but four of the groups for the 1984 survey.

Results of Poverty Estimates

Extreme Poverty

Table 4.1 presents the results of the estimates for extreme poverty rates for 1984, 1989, 1992 and 1994.[10] The estimates reveal a consistent pattern for the distribution of poverty between urban and rural areas. Within each survey year, the prevalence of poverty is much higher in rural areas than in urban areas (Table 4.1). In 1984, 18.3 per cent of the population fell below the extreme poverty line, but the rate of extreme poverty was much greater in rural areas, where 34.5 per cent of the population was extremely poor, than in urban areas, where only 9.0 per cent of the population was extremely poor. Nearly 70 per cent of the extremely poor were located in rural areas.

In 1989, 1992 and 1994 the head count measures for extreme poverty reflect a similar pattern with rural poverty rates four to five time greater than urban poverty rates, and with the contribution of the rural areas to the overall poverty rate exceeding 75 per cent.

The PPG, which reflects the intensity of poverty among the poor, presents a similar picture. While the overall measure of poverty for the PPG in 1984 is 0.057, the rate for rural poverty, 0.115, is much higher than the 0.023 rate for urban poverty. Indeed, at 75.4 per cent, the contribution of rural areas to the overall poverty rate is even higher for the PPG than for the head count index. The estimates for the PPG for the other survey years follow this same pattern. The rates for extreme poverty in rural areas are much higher than in urban areas, and the contribution of the rural areas to the overall poverty level is greater when the intensity of the poverty, that is the income shortfall of the poor, is accounted for.

The FGT measure, which takes into consideration the distribution of expenditure among the poor, reflects an even greater contribution by rural areas to the overall poverty rate. In each survey year, the estimate for rural poverty was much higher than the estimate for urban poverty. The contribution of rural areas to the overall poverty level was also greater for the FGT measure than for either the HC or the PPG measures for each survey year; this greater contribution of the rural areas suggests greater inequality among the rural poor.

Moderate Poverty

Table 4.2 presents the results of the estimates of moderate poverty rates for 1984, 1989, 1992 and 1994. As with the estimates for extreme poverty rates, the estimates of moderate poverty rates reveal a consistent pattern in the distribution of poverty between urban and rural areas. The proportion of the rural population falling below the moderate poverty line ranges from 90.4 per cent to 93.7 per cent and is higher than that of the proportion of the urban population falling below the poverty line, which ranges from 63.7 per cent to 72.2 per cent, for each survey year. However, the gap between the proportion of the rural and urban populations in moderate poverty is much smaller than the gap for extreme poverty. In each survey year, over 90 per cent of the rural population was moderately poor, while the rate for urban poverty ranged from 63.7 per cent to 72.2 per cent. In contrast to the case of extreme poverty, an overwhelming majority of the moderately poor are not found in rural areas. The proportion of the moderately poor who reside in rural areas was roughly one half, varying from 41.9 per cent to 52.2 per cent.

The estimates of the PPG for moderate poverty also indicate that poverty is much more intense in rural areas than in urban areas. The PPG for rural areas varied from 0.584 to 0.623 while the PPG for urban areas was considerably lower, varying from 0.288 to 0.351. In each of the survey years, the contribution of rural poverty was greater for the PPG measure than for the HC measure. This suggests that the poorest of the moderately poor are concentrated in rural areas. This result is consistent with the estimates of extreme poverty which indicate that the bulk of the extremely poor were concentrated in rural areas.

The estimates of the FGT measure also reflect the greater severity of poverty in rural areas. The estimates of the FGT for rural areas were much higher then the estimates for urban areas for each survey year. The contribution of rural areas to the overall poverty rate was greater than that of the urban areas. In each year, the contribution of rural areas to the overall poverty level was also greater for the FGT measure than for either the HC or the PPG measures; this suggests that there is greater inequality among the rural poor.

Changes in Poverty Rates 1984-1994

The absolute and per cent changes in the rates for extreme and moderate poverty for 1984-89, 1989-82 and 1992-94 are presented in Tables 4.3 and 4.4.

1984 to 1989

The situation in rural areas seems to have deteriorated considerably from 1984 to 1989 as both extreme and moderate poverty rates increased markedly. In particular, the estimates for extreme poverty reveal that there was a significant increase in the extent of poverty from 1984 to 1989 as the HC index for the nation increased by 2.8 percentage points (Table 4.3).[11] This increase in the rate of poverty occurred at a time of rapid population growth which implies an even larger increase in the number of individuals living in extreme poverty (Table 4.5).

   The increase in the rate of extreme poverty at the national level does not reflect a general decline in consumption throughout society, but rather was due to the sharp increase in extreme poverty in rural areas. The percentage of the rural population falling below the extreme poverty line increased 6.3 percentage points (Table 4.3), from 34.5 per cent to 40.8 per cent (Table 4.1); while at the same time there was no significant change in the rate of extreme poverty in urban areas.

   Changes in poverty rates measured by the PPG follow a similar pattern for this time period. The PPG for the nation increased by 21.1 per cent (Table 4.4). The increase in the PPG at the national level was caused by a large increase, 27.0 per cent, in the PPG for rural areas, while there was no significant change in the PPG for urban areas.

   The FGT measure of extreme poverty for 1984 and 1989 also reveals a worsening of poverty at the national level and in rural areas. The FGT index increased by 28.0 per cent at the national level and by 34.0 per cent at the rural level. There was no significant change for urban areas.

   For this same time period, the results for moderate poverty present a much different picture than those for extreme poverty. There was no significant change in the extent, depth or severity of moderate poverty at the national level from 1984 to 1989. There were, however, significant changes in the poverty rates for both rural and urban areas. For each of the poverty measures estimated, there was a significant increase in the rate of moderate rural poverty, and, at the same time, a significant decrease in the rate of moderate urban poverty. The combination of these contradictory movements in the rural and urban poverty rates left the national poverty rate virtually unchanged. However, because of the rapidly growing population, the roughly constant poverty rate implies a large increase in the number of moderately poor individuals (Table 4.5).

At first blush it may seem somewhat surprising that the rate of moderate poverty decreased given that per capita GDP fell by 5.1 per cent during this period. A strong positive relationship between growth and poverty reduction is widely accepted in the development literature. However, growth in per capita GDP is not a precise indicator of how the purchasing power of the poor is changing.[12] In the model which underlies the identification of the poor in this study, per capita household expenditure, and not per capita GDP, is the determinant of poverty. Changes in per capita GDP will not reflect changes in certain factors which determine household expenditures, like the allocation of household income between savings and consumption. In a recessionary economy, households near the poverty line will tend to decrease their rate of savings in order to maintain consumption levels. Table 4.6 reveals that just such a decrease in the savings rate occurred in Mexico from 1984 to 1989. The decrease in the savings rate allowed for a much smaller decrease in per capita private consumption than in per capita GDP. The relatively small decline in per capita consumption partially explains how Mexico was able to avoid an increase in moderate poverty rates, but the fall in savings which made it possible does not bode well for long run poverty reduction.

1989 to 1992

The trend in the poverty rates changed between 1989 and 1992 as there was a general improvement in the lot of the poor with extreme and moderate poverty rates declining for both urban and rural areas. For this time period, the HC index for extreme poverty for the nation fell by 1.3 percentage points. This improvement in the national level poverty rate was driven by a large fall, 2.9 percentage points, in the rural poverty rate; while there was a smaller, one percentage point decrease in the urban HC index. It is important to note, however, that despite this improvement, the national rate for extreme poverty in 1992 was still higher than in 1984. This was due primarily to the sharp increase in extreme poverty in rural areas from 1984 to 1989, which the general improvement from 1989 to 1992 did not fully erase.

For the PPG and FGT indices there were slight, but not significant, decreases in poverty at the national level. There were significant changes in the urban FGT, and in the rural areas where there was a 12.3 per cent decrease in the PPG index and a 15.5 per cent decrease in the FGT index. This would suggest an improvement in the lot of the poorest of the poor.

Moderate poverty rates for the 1989 to 1992 period were uniformly decreasing, and were actually lower in 1992 than in 1984 . The HC index for the nation fell by 3.0 percentage points. This decline in national poverty was led by the decrease in the extent of poverty in urban areas, where the HC index fell by 4.3 percentage points. Rural poverty also showed a significant decline for this period, but the magnitude of the decline, 1.5 percentage points, was much smaller. Although the rural moderate poverty rate was still higher in 1992 than in 1984, the continued decline in the urban moderate poverty rate drove the national rate for moderate poverty well below its 1984 level.

The PPG and FGT indices also fell for the 1989 to 1992 time period. The PPG index fell by 5.3 per cent at the national level with both the rural and urban areas experiencing significant decreases in poverty (Table 4.4). The FGT index declined by 9.6 per cent, and both the rural and urban areas also experienced significant declines.

1992 to 1994

From 1992 to 1994 the rates for both extreme and moderate poverty showed very little change. At the national level, the HC index experienced a slight increase, and the PPG and FGT indices fell slightly; however, none of these changes was large enough to be statistically significant. The only significant change in extreme poverty was for the FGT index for rural areas. There was a small, but significant, decline in the FGT index for rural areas indicating some improvement in the distribution of expenditure among the extremely poor. The estimates for moderate poverty for this time period also reveal very little change. For all three measures there was a small, but not statistically significant increase in the poverty rates at the national, rural and urban levels.

Summary of Poverty Changes - 1984 to 1994

As the last year of economic growth before the peso crisis radically altered the macroeconomic situation once again, 1994 provides a convenient breaking point to assess the initial effects of the adjustment process. The lack of significant changes between 1992 and 1994 left both extreme and moderate rural poverty rates for 1994 lower than their peak in

1989, but still much higher than at the beginning of the adjustment period. Because most of the extremely poor are in rural areas, the deteriorating situation in rural areas caused the national rate for extreme poverty to increase over the adjustment period as well.

In contrast, urban poverty rates experienced a decline over the adjustment period. The larger share of urban households among the moderately poor caused the moderate poverty rate to fall. Nevertheless, it is important to note that these changes occurred during a period of rapid population expansion. The rapid population growth combined with the higher rates of extreme poverty to increase the number of extremely poor individuals by almost five million. The rapid population growth also more than offset the improvement in moderate poverty rates as the number of moderately poor increased by almost thirteen million.

It should also be noted that these large increases in the number of poor individuals occurred during a subset of the entire adjustment period. The implementation of some adjustment policies began shortly after the debt crisis in 1984, before the first year for which comparable household level income-expenditure data are available. The decline in per capita income from 1982 to 1984 makes it likely that the number of poor had already begun to increase before the first year of this study. This implies that the results of the study probably understate the increase in poverty associated with the adjustment policies and external shocks which occurred over this period.

Comparison with other Studies

Although the vast majority of studies of poverty in Mexico are for a single period and do not allow comparison over time, there are two recent studies which contain brief looks at how poverty changed over time.

In a 1991 World Bank study, Levy (1991) estimated the incidence of poverty in Mexico using data from the 1984 ENIGH. The World Bank study used per capita expenditure to estimate the FGT family of poverty indices, and found that approximately 19.5 per cent of the population could be classified as extremely poor and 81.2 per cent as moderately poor according to the head count index.

As part of a 1993 study of changes in income distribution in Mexico, Alarcon (1994) also measured changes in poverty between 1984 and 1989. Alarcon used data on household expenditure from the ENIGH, and in order to make her results comparable with those of Levy, replicated his methodology.[13] Although Alarcon did not independently estimate poverty rates for 1984, the methodology she followed should allow her results to be compared with the World Bank results for 1984. Because of the similarity of the methodology and the data used, the comparison of the poverty rates estimated in these two studies should be similar to my estimates of the changes in poverty rates between 1984 and 1989.

The changes in extreme poverty implied by the studies of the World Bank and Alarcon are indeed roughly similar to my estimates. Both the World Bank/Alarcon results and my own suggest large increases in extreme poverty at the rural and national levels. There is a small difference in the results for urban areas where the World Bank/Alarcon results show a slight increase in urban poverty, while my results show a slight, though not significant, decline in urban poverty.

The results for moderate poverty, however, are not nearly as similar. Both the World Bank/Alarcon and my study show a fairly large decrease in urban poverty, but the World Bank/Alarcon studies imply a large decrease in rural poverty, while my estimates suggest a large increase in rural poverty. Both studies show a decrease in the national poverty level, though my estimates show a much smaller decrease.

The results suggested by the World Bank/Alarcon studies in this case are somewhat perplexing. In particular, the behavior of the national HC index is difficult to explain given the changes in the HC indices for rural and urban areas. The national HC index is just a weighted average of the urban and rural HC indices, with the weights given by the proportion of population in the urban and rural areas. The studies of the World Bank and Alarcon imply that the rural HC index decreased by 3.9 percentage points (a four per cent decline), the urban HC index decreased by 2.1 percentage points (a 2.9 per cent decline), and the national HC index decreased by 1.9 percentage points (a 2.4 per cent decline). As a weighted average of the rural and urban HC indices, the national HC index cannot have decreased by less than both the rural and urban indices. This discrepancy suggests that there must be some inconsistency, perhaps in the data handling, between the two studies.

In addition to the World Bank/Alarcon studies, the Economic Commission for Latin America and the Caribbean has also studied the extent of poverty in Mexico. The ECLAC study used data on per capita income from the 1984, 1989 and 1992 to estimate a series of poverty indices. Since the ECLAC study employed a consistent methodology and data handling, it should not suffer from the apparent inconsistencies between the Levy and Alarcon studies. Because the ECLAC study used income per capita which was adjusted for underreporting, and different poverty lines, the poverty rates for a given year are not comparable to mine. However, the changes in poverty rates over time should follow the same general pattern.

The ECLAC estimates of extreme poverty for 1984 and 1989 suggest that the extent of poverty increased at the national, rural and urban levels. The ECLAC estimates for moderate poverty also show an increase at the national, rural and urban levels. For the 1989 to 1992 period, the ECLAC study shows a large decrease in extreme poverty at all levels. The stimates for moderate poverty reveal a decrease in the national and urban rates, and no change in moderate rural poverty.

These results for 1989 and 1992 are similar to mine estimates. The results for the change from 1984 to 1989, however, differ in their suggestion that both extreme and moderate urban poverty increased. Our estimates for this same time period show a decrease in both extreme and moderate urban poverty. This discrepancy is somewhat surprising given that the ECLAC study's indication that extreme and moderate rural poverty increased is consistent with results of this study. A possible explanation for the discrepancy may be differences in the adjustment made to the data for agricultural and non-agricultural income for underreporting.

Robustness of Results

The differences in the results of the various studies suggest that some care must be taken in drawing detailed conclusions about the way in which poverty has changed over time. Differences in the data handling and selection of poverty lines and poverty measures may have strong effects on the perceived trends in the evolution of poverty. The extreme sensitivity of the poverty estimates to the choice of poverty line is due to the fact that the poverty lines for developing countries are typically quite close to the mode of the income (or expenditure) distribution. In this case, the mode of the 1984 expenditure distribution falls at approximately 11,000 pesos per quarter,[14] quite close to the extreme poverty line of 7,742 pesos per quarter[15] (see Charts 4.1-4.3). Indeed, if the extreme poverty line for 1989 were defined as 185,000 pesos per quarter,[16] just seven per cent lower than the extreme poverty line actually used, the 1989 head count index would have the same value as the 1984 head count index, and we would have to change the conclusion that poverty had increased during this period. This extreme sensitivity to the poverty line thus highlights the importance of proper deflation when making intertemporal comparisons of poverty, as relatively small differences in price indices may have relatively large impacts on the poverty estimates. More generally, any distributionally neutral change in the measured income level, whether caused by an actual change in income level or improper deflation, will have a large effect on poverty estimates.

The proximity of the poverty lines to the mode of the distribution, and the sensitivity of the poverty rates to the measures used requires that great care be used in interpreting the results of intertemporal poverty estimates. In order to assess whether the qualitative results given above are robust to the choice of poverty line and poverty measure, the cumulative frequency distributions for expenditure are given in Charts 4.4-4.7.

It can be seen from Chart 4.4 that the first order dominance condition does not hold for 1984 and 1989. This implies that different poverty lines may yield different conclusions about the direction of change in poverty rates. It is particularly important to note that the cumulative distributions cross at an expenditure level just beyond the level of the moderate poverty line. If an appreciably higher moderate poverty line has been employed, the conclusion that moderate poverty rates increased may have been reversed. While the methodology used to define the moderate poverty line is quite sound, it must be emphasized that a different conception of the level of consumption necessary to escape moderate poverty could present a different picture of the evolution of poverty between these two years.

No such ambiguity exists for the 1989 to 1992 time period. The 1989 distribution lies entirely to the left of the 1992 distribution, indicating that the first order dominance condition holds for the 1989 and 1992 cumulative expenditure distributions. This implies that any poverty line and all well-behaved poverty measures will indicate an decrease in poverty between the two years.

The first order dominance condition does not hold for the 1992 and 1994 distributions. As such, any conclusions regarding qualitative changes in the poverty rate may be sensitive to the poverty line or poverty measure. Of greater interest are the cumulative distributions for 1984 and 1994. Importantly, first order dominance does not hold for these distributions either. From Chart 4.7 it can be seen that that the 1984 distribution is well above the 1994 distribution at higher expenditure levels, but that the opposite is true at lower distributions. This highlights the important difference in the changes in the extreme and moderate poverty rates over the entire period of the study. While moderate poverty improved, ranks of the poorest of the poor swelled.

Growth-Inequality Decomposition of Changes in Poverty

In addition to affecting the rate of poverty, adjustment policies are also likely to have an impact on the distribution of income within an adjusting country. In general, changes in the rate of poverty are due to a combination of changes in the mean level of expenditure and in the distribution of expenditure. Other things being equal, an increase (decrease) in the mean expenditure of a given population will always reduce (increase) its poverty rate. In most cases, an decrease (increase) in the level of inequality will also reduce (increase) the poverty rate.[17] Changes in mean expenditure and expenditure distribution may counteract one another or work in conjunction. The changes in poverty rates reported in the previous sections are the result of both changes in the mean level of expenditure and in inequality.

Just as there is no simple relationship between adjustment and poverty, the way in which inequality will respond to adjustment is also difficult to predict due to the differing effects of different components of adjustment programs. One possible result is an improvement in inequality due to the liberalization of trade policies. The elimination of trade policies designed to decrease the cost of importing capital goods should shift the factor mix toward more labor intensive production. More labor intensive production should increase wages and decrease inequality. Another possibility is suggested by Feszbein and Psacharopoulos's study of adjusting countries in Latin America. Feszbein and Psacharopoulos (1995) found evidence of a strong negative correlation between changes in income and inequality. This implies that if the contractionary policies associated with the initial stages of adjustment cause income to fall, a deterioration of the distribution of income would also occur. The increase in inequality would exacerbate the effect of the fall in income, and poverty rates would be likely to fall considerably.

An estimate of the extent to which changes in mean expenditure and the distribution of expenditure were responsible for the changes in poverty in this study can be made by decomposing the changes into their growth and redistribution components.[18] The FGT family of poverty indices are a function of the poverty line (z), mean per capita expenditures (μ) and the inequality of expenditure. The inequality of expenditure may be represented by a Lorenz curve.[19] If the Lorenz curve is represented by the function $L(s)$ with k parameters $m_1, m_2, \ldots m_k$, which determine the level of inequality, then the FGT poverty measures for time t can be written as:

(1) $P_{\alpha t}=P(z,\ \mu_t, L(s)_t)$.

This implies:

(2) $dP_{\alpha t} = \dfrac{\partial P_{\alpha t}}{\partial \mu} d\mu + \displaystyle\sum_{i=1}^{k} \dfrac{\partial P_{\alpha t}}{\partial L} \dfrac{\partial L}{\partial m_i} dm_i$

The first term on the right hand side of equation *2* indicates the impact of changes in mean expenditure on poverty holding the distribution of expenditure constant. The second term indicates the impact on poverty of a change in the distribution of expenditure holding the mean expenditure constant.

Changes in the rates of Mexican poverty were decomposed into their growth and redistribution components using the following procedure: The poverty measure for time period *t+1* was recalculated assuming that the distribution of expenditure in time period *t+1* had not changed from time period *t*, but that the mean expenditure had changed. The growth component of the change in time period *t* to time period *t+1* is defined then as : $P^*_{\alpha t+1} - P_{\alpha t}$, where $P^*_{\alpha t+1}$ is the poverty measure calculated at in time period *t+1* assuming no change in the distribution. The inequality component is defined as the difference between the total percentage change in poverty and the growth component:

$\left(P_{\alpha t+1} - P_{\alpha t}\right) - \left(P^*_{\alpha t+1} - P_{\alpha t}\right)$.

The results of the growth-inequality decomposition for moderate poverty are presented in Table 4.7. From 1984 to 1989 the extent of rural poverty increased by 3.3 percentage points. If the distribution of expenditure had remained the same between the two years, the poverty index would have increased by only 2.4 percentage points. However, the increase in inequality over the period exacerbated the effect of the fall in mean expenditure, and the poverty rate increased by an additional 0.7 percentage points. The urban head count index fell by 4.2 percentage points and the national head count index by 0.7 percentage points during this time period. However, had the distribution of expenditure remained the same, the rate of poverty for both would have decreased by even more, falling by 8.0 percentage points for urban areas and 1.4 percentage points for the nation. The increase in inequality partially offset the gains from the increase in mean expenditure and poverty rates fell by only about one half as much as they would have had the distribution not changed.

It may seem somewhat surprising that the effect of increased inequality was not greater over this period. Alarcon (1994) and Fujii and Aguilar (1995) both report large increases in income inequality from 1984 to 1989. Both studies used the Gini coefficient as their measure of inequality. Changes in inequality are most commonly characterized by changes in some summary statistic like the Gini coefficient. However, these summary statistics measure inequality over the entire distribution and may not be helpful in determining the effect of changes in inequality on changes in poverty. The changes in inequality which are most likely to have an effect on poverty are changes in the distribution near the poverty line. Summary statistics weight changes anywhere in the distribution equally and may not reflect the important changes near the poverty line. For example, the large increase in the Gini coefficient between 1984 and 1989 would lead one to expect that the redistribution effect would greatly exacerbate the fall in mean expenditure. However, much of this increase in the Gini coefficient was due to a sharp increase in the income of the wealthiest decile far above the poverty line (see Table 4.8), and the contribution of the increase in inequality to the increase in poverty was in fact smaller that the contribution of the fall in mean expenditure.

From 1989 to 1992 the extent of rural poverty fell by 1.5 percentage points. Had the distribution of expenditure not improved over the relevant range, the fall in poverty would have been only two fifths as large.[20] The poverty rates for the urban and national levels fell by 4.3 and 2.8 percentage points. However, a small increase in inequality over the relevant range of the distribution caused these improvements to be slightly smaller, seven per cent for the urban area and three per cent for the nation, than they would have been had the distribution remained constant.

From 1992 to 1994 the head count index for all areas showed small, but not significant increases. For all three areas, the fall in per capita expenditure was responsible for most of the increase, while a small increase in inequality reinforced the growth effect.

Thus, as can be seen from Table 4.7, the growth component dominates the redistribution component in all cases except for the change in rural poverty from 1989 to 1992. The increase in inequality in 1989 exacerbated the primary effect of falling per capita expenditure. In 1992 a slight increase in urban and national inequality only slightly mitigated the effect of increasing per capita expenditure, but in rural areas the improved distribution was the most important factor in decreasing poverty. In 1994 the small decrease in inequality offset a small fraction of the increase in poverty due to the decline in mean expenditure.

Conclusions

The results of the poverty estimates reported above reveal that certain broad characteristics of the poverty profile of Mexico have remained unchanged over the period of adjustment. Most notably, throughout the adjustment period, extreme poverty has remained primarily a rural phenomenon - roughly one fifth of the population lives in extreme poverty. The great majority of those in extreme poverty are rural dwellers, and rural dwellers are much more likely than urban dwellers to live in extreme poverty. The concentration of extreme poverty in rural areas is even more pronounced when the income shortfalls of the poor and the inequality among the poor are accounted for.

Within this broadly consistent pattern of poverty, however, there have also been significant changes over the adjustment period. The most important changes have been the large increase in the absolute number of individuals living in poverty and the difference between the evolution of rural and urban poverty rates. Over the entire period of study, the proportion of individuals living in extreme poverty showed only a small increase; but this increase occurred in the context of a rapidly growing population and resulted in an absolute increase of almost five million extremely poor individuals over the course of the adjustment period.

From 1984 to 1989 the situation in rural areas deteriorated considerably as poverty rates increased sharply, and the poor fell farther below the poverty line. There was a relatively small improvement in rural poverty rate from 1989 to 1992, and a slight deterioration from 1992 to 1994. However, even after the improvement after 1989, the poverty rate was still worse in the later years than in 1984. This suggests that after increasing sharply in the initial stage of adjustment, rural poverty rates improved somewhat, but still remained considerably higher than they were prior to adjustment. The number of rural poor did not improve after the initial sharp increase, and the net increase for the adjustment period was over five million.

In urban areas, there appears to have been a general improvement in the rate of poverty from 1984 through 1992 before a slight, but not significant, increase in poverty in 1994. In 1994 the rates still remained much lower than they had been in 1984, and the number of poor in urban areas was roughly the same in 1994 as it was at the beginning of adjustment. The difference in the trend in poverty rates for urban and rural areas is highlighted by the fraction of the poor found in each region: during the adjustment period the fraction of the poor who dwell in rural areas increased markedly. Thus, it appears that the adjustment process favored urban, as opposed to rural, dwellers at the low end of the distribution.

In assessing the impact of adjustment on poverty, it is important to note that the date of the initial survey, 1984, was after the onset of the debt crisis and the subsequent beginning of the adjustment process in Mexico. By the time of the first survey, per capita income had already begun to fall. Therefore it is very likely that poverty rates had begun to increase before the survey was administered in 1984. As such, the increase in the number of poor over the adjustment period may have been even greater than the results of this study indicate.

The examination of the relative importance of growth and inequality in determining how the rate of poverty evolved reveals that the changes in poverty were driven more by changes in the mean level of expenditure than by changes in inequality. Although there were significant changes in the distribution if expenditure over the period of adjustment, much of the change occurred at income levels well above the poverty line and so did not have a strong effect on poverty.

Table 4.1:   Extreme Poverty Rates: 1984, 1989, 1992, 1994

	Head Count	Percent of all Poor	Poverty Gap	Percent of all PG	FGT	Percent of all FGT
1984						
Rural	0.345	68.9	0.115	74.4	0.053	77.7
Urban	0.090	31.1	0.023	25.6	0.009	22.3
National	0.183	100.0	0.057	100.0	0.025	100.0
1989						
Rural	0.408	75.3	0.146	82.2	0.071	85.8
Urban	0.085	24.7	0.020	17.8	0.008	14.2
National	0.211	100.0	0.069	100.0	0.032	100.0
1992						
Rural	0.379	81.0	0.128	85.4	0.060	87.9
Urban	0.075	19.0	0.015	14.6	0.006	12.1
National	0.200	100.0	0.065	100.0	0.029	100.0
1994						
Rural	0.384	79.3	0.123	83.5	0.054	85.9
Urban	0.073	20.7	0.018	16.5	0.006	14.1
National	0.203	100.0	0.062	100.0	0.027	100.0

Source: Author's calculations based on ENIGH, various years.

Table 4.2: Moderate Poverty Rates: 1984, 1989, 1992, 1994

	Head Count	Percent of all Poor	Poverty Gap	Percent of all PG	FGT	Percent of all FGT
1984						
Rural	0.904	41.9	0.584	51.0	0.421	53.7
Urban	0.722	58.1	0.351	49.0	0.209	46.3
National	0.788	100.0	0.447	100.0	0.294	100.0
1989						
Rural	0.937	46.8	0.623	55.2	0.454	60.7
Urban	0.680	53.2	0.322	44.8	0.188	39.3
National	0.781	100.0	0.440	100.0	0.292	100.0
1992						
Rural	0.922	52.2	0.590	60.4	0.418	65.8
Urban	0.637	47.8	0.288	39.6	0.162	34.2
National	0.754	100.0	0.417	100.0	0.264	100.0
1994						
Rural	0.931	50.8	0.599	59.7	0.424	65.0
Urban	0.653	49.2	0.294	40.3	0.165	35.0
National	0.769	100.0	0.424	100.0	0.269	100.0

Source: Author's calculations based on ENIGH, various years.

Table 4.3:   Change in Poverty Rates over Time: 1984-1994

		EXTREME POVERTY		
		HEAD COUNT	POVERTY GAP	FGT
1984-1989	Rural	.063*	.031*	.018*
	Urban	-.005	-.003	-.001
	National	.028*	.012*	.007*
1989-1992	Rural	-.029*	-.018*	-.011*
	Urban	-.010*	-.005	-.002*
	National	-.013*	-.004	-.003
1992-1994	Rural	.005	-.005	-.006*
	Urban	-.002	.003	.000
	National	.003	-.003	-.002
1984-1994	Rural	.039*	.008	.001
	Urban	-.017	-.005+	-.003*
	National	.020	.005	.002

Table 4.3: Continued

		MODERATE POVERTY		
		HEAD COUNT	POVERTY GAP	FGT
1984-1989	Rural	.033*	.039*	.033*
	Urban	-.042*	-.029*	-.021*
	National	-.007	-.007	-.002
1989-1992	Rural	-.015*	-.032*	-.036*
	Urban	-.043*	-.034*	-.026*
	National	-.030*	-.033*	-.028*
1992-1994	Rural	.009	.009	.006
	Urban	.016	.006	.003
	National	.015	.007	.005
1984-1994	Rural	.027*	.015	.003
	Urban	-.069*	-.055*	-.044*
	National	-.019	-.023+	-.025*

Source: Author's calculations from ENIGH, various years.
Note: Asterisks indicate changes which are significant at the 5% confidence level.

Table 4.4:   Percent Change in Poverty Rates: 1984-1994

		EXTREME POVERTY		
		HEAD COUNT	POVERTY GAP	FGT
1984-1989	Rural	18.3*	27.0*	34.0*
	Urban	-5.6	-13.0	-11.1
	National	15.3*	21.1*	28.0*
1989-1992	Rural	-7.1*	-12.3*	-15.5*
	Urban	-11.7*	-20.0	-25.5*
	National	-5.5*	-7.2	-9.4
1992-1994	Rural	1.3	-3.9	-10.0
	Urban	-2.7	12.5	0.0
	National	1.5	-3.1	-6.9
1984-1994	Rural	11.2*	7.0	1.9
	Urban	-18.9	-21.7[+]	-33.3*
	National	10.9	8.8	8.0

Table 4.4: Continued

		MODERATE POVERTY		
		HEAD COUNT	POVERTY GAP	FGT
1984-1989	Rural	3.7*	6.7*	7.8*
	Urban	-5.8*	-8.3*	-10.0*
	National	-0.8	-1.6	-0.7
1989-1992	Rural	-1.6*	-5.2*	-7.9*
	Urban	-6.3*	-10.6*	-13.8*
	National	-3.5*	-5.3*	-9.6*
1992-1994	Rural	0.9	1.5	1.4
	Urban	2.5	2.1	1.9
	National	2.1	1.7	1.8
1984-1994	Rural	2.9*	2.6	0.7
	Urban	-9.6*	-17.1*	-21.0*
	National	-2.4	-5.1+	-8.5*

Source: *Author's calculations from ENIGH, various years.*
Note: *Asterisks indicate changes which are significant at the 5% confidence level.*

Table 4.5: Number of Individuals Living in Poverty

National	Extreme Poverty	Moderate Poverty
1984	13,140,472	56,583,020
1989	16,698,743	61,809,094
1992	16,857,005	63,550,989
1994	18,222,086	69,028,493
Rural	**Extreme Poverty**	**Moderate Poverty**
1984	9,142,501	23,950,000
1989	12,321,599	28,297,360
1992	13,037,650	31,716,800
1994	14,360,386	34,484,793
Urban	**Extreme Poverty**	**Moderate Poverty**
1984	3,997,971	32,633,020
1989	4,377,144	33,511,734
1992	3,819,355	31,834,189
1994	3,861,700	34,543,700

Source: Author's calculations from ENIGH, various years.

Table 4.6: Macroeconomic Indicators: 1980-1994

	Real GDP per capita[a]	Real Private Cons. per capita[b]	Savings Rate[c]
1980	6,671	5,011	14.6
1981	7,087	5,274	14.6
1982	6,882	5,058	14.9
1983	6,447	4,727	15.2
1984	6,542	4,815	13.3
1985	6,577	4,867	13.2
1986	6,214	4,674	4.9
1987	6,215	4,575	9.7
1988	6,188	4,565	8.6
1989	6,285	4,742	9.4
1990	6,453	4,918	10.4
1991	6,558	5,053	9.3
1992	6,607	5,135	7.2
1993	6,527	5,056	6.4
1994	6,749	5,230	--
Cumulative Change 1984-89 (%)	-3.9	-1.4	--
Cumulative Change 1989-92 (%)	5.1	8.3	--
Cumulative Change 1992-94 (%)	2.1	1.8	--

a   *1980 pesos. Source: La Economía Mexicana en Cifras.*
b   *1980 pesos. Source: Cuentas Nacionales de México, various years.*
c   *Percentages. Source: Cuentas Nacionales de México, various years.*

Table 4.7: Growth-Equity Decomposition for Moderate Poverty: 1984-1994

	1984 - 1989		
	Percentage Change in Head Count Index	Growth Effect	Redistribution Effect
Rural	-.033	.024	.007
Urban	-.042	-.080	.038
National	-.007	-.014	.007

	1989 - 1992		
	Percentage Change in Head Count Index	Growth Effect	Redistribution Effect
Rural	-.015	.006	-.009
Urban	-.043	-.046	.003
National	-.027	-.028	.001

	1992 - 1994		
	Percentage Change in Head Count Index	Growth Effect	Redistribution Effect
Rural	.009	.013	-.004
Urban	.018	.020	-.002
National	.015	.019	-.004

Source: Author's calculations based on ENIGH, various years.

Table 4.8: Decile Means for Per Capita Expenditure: 1984-1994

Decile	1984	1989	1992	1994	Percent Change 1984-89	Percent Change 1989-92	Percent Change 1992-94
1	4,156	4,020	4,349	4,662	-3.3	8.2	-0.7
2	6,935	6,791	7,273	7,369	-2.1	7.1	1.3
3	9,412	9,230	9,753	9,846	-1.9	5.7	1.0
4	11,941	11,753	12,432	12,449	-1.6	5.7	0.0
5	14,875	14,563	15,506	15,376	-2.1	6.5	-0.8
6	18,398	18,128	19,372	18,991	-1.5	6.8	-2.0
7	22,938	22,782	24,160	23,970	0.7	6.0	-0.8
8	29,298	29,670	31,553	31,027	1.3	6.3	-1.7
9	40,913	42,295	45,156	44,872	3.4	6.7	-0.6
10	96,973	111,691	117,996	118,160	15.2	5.6	0.0
Mean	31,799	33,080	36,120	35860			

Source: Author's calculations from *ENIGH*, various years.
Note: Means are in 1984 pesos.

Table 4.9: Decile Means for Urban Per Capita Expenditure: 1984-1994

Decile	1984	1989	1992	1994	Percent Change 1984-89	Percent Change 1989-92	Percent Change 1992-94
1	6,023	6,606	7,366	7,447	9.6	11.5	-1.1
2	9,747	10,445	11,510	11,629	7.1	10.2	1.0
3	12,613	13,486	14,735	14,873	6.9	9.2	0.9
4	15,506	16,580	18,367	18,133	5.0	10.7	-1.3
5	18,802	20,059	22,176	22,078	6.7	10.6	-0.4
6	22,883	24,482	26,688	26,537	7.0	9.0	-0.6
7	27,842	30,189	33,114	32,601	8.4	9.7	-1.5
8	35,123	38,702	42,343	42,166	10.2	9.4	-0.4
9	48,281	53,656	60,445	60,557	11.1	12.7	0.2
10	107,029	136,277	149,420	150,169	27.3	9.6	0.5
Mean	36,980	42,200	47,540	46,760			

Source: *Author's calculations from ENIGH, various years.*
Note: *Means are in 1984 pesos.*

Table 4.10: Decile Means for Rural Per Capita Expenditure: 1984-1994

Decile	1984	1989	1992	1994	Percent Change 1984-89	Percent Change 1989-92	Percent Change 1992-94
1	3,211	2,876	3,290	3,667	-10.4	14.4	11.5
2	4,873	4,695	5,171	5,437	-3.7	10.1	5.1
3	6,309	5,915	6,630	6,754	-6.2	12.1	1.9
4	7,822	7,342	8,058	8,177	-6.1	5.6	1.5
5	9,567	8,900	9,647	9,714	-6.9	8.4	-2.6
6	11,609	10,682	11,656	11,523	-7.9	9.1	-1.1
7	14,482	12,787	14,264	13,841	-11.7	14.3	-3.0
8	18,662	15,873	17,825	17,035	-15.4	12.3	-4.4
9	25,914	21,542	23,646	22,770	-16.8	9.7	-3.7
10	66,692	48,281	52,186	51,850	-27.6	8.1	-6.4
Mean	22,300	16,720	18,840	18,720			

Source: Author's calculations from *ENIGH, various years.*
Note: Means are in *1984 pesos.*

Chart 4.1: Distribution of Expenditure: 1984, 1989

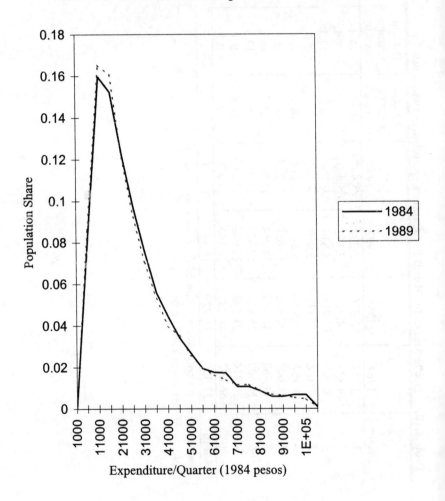

Chart 4.2: Distribution of Expenditure: 1989, 1992

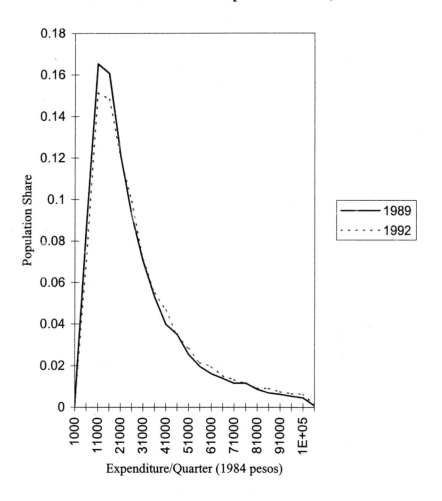

Chart 4.3: Distribution of Expenditure: 1992, 1994

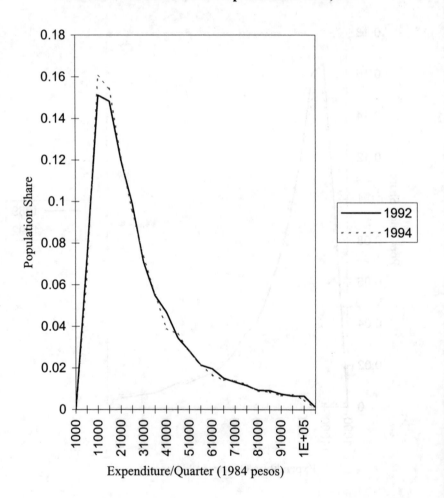

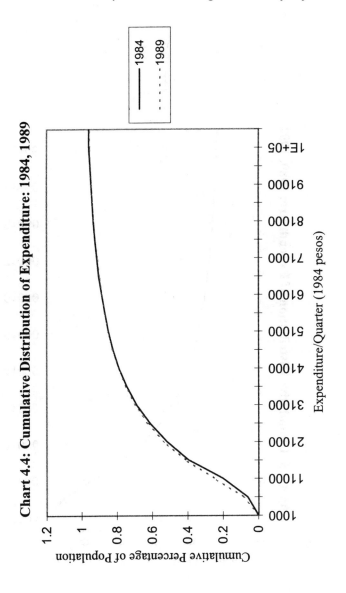

Chart 4.4: Cumulative Distribution of Expenditure: 1984, 1989

1984

1989

Cumulative Percentage of Population

Expenditure/Quarter (1984 pesos)

1000 11000 21000 31000 41000 51000 61000 71000 81000 91000 1E+05

0 0.2 0.4 0.6 0.8 1 1.2

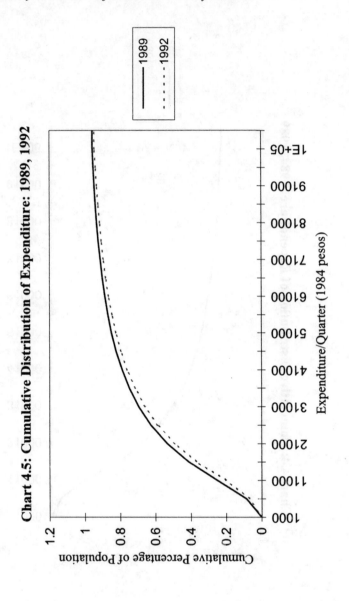

Chart 4.5: Cumulative Distribution of Expenditure: 1989, 1992

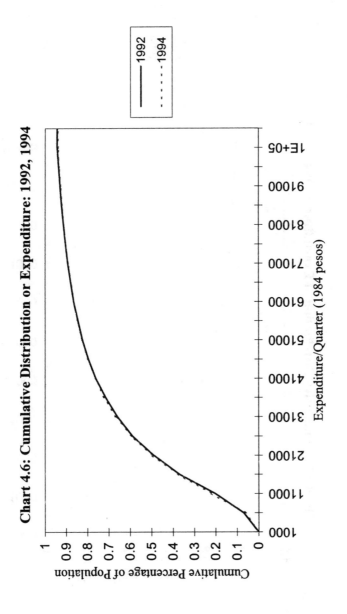

Chart 4.6: Cumulative Distribution or Expenditure: 1992, 1994

1992
1994

Cumulative Percentage of Population

Expenditure/Quarter (1984 pesos)

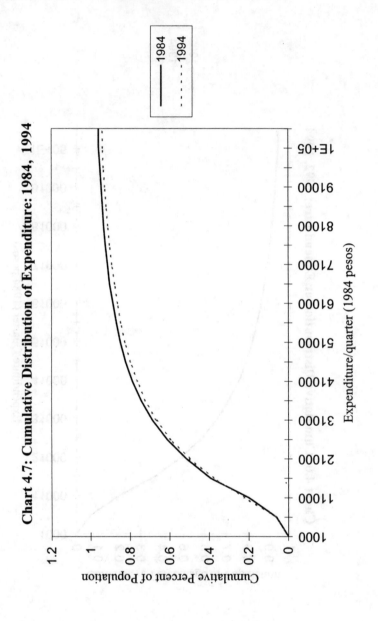

Chart 4.7: Cumulative Distribution of Expenditure: 1984, 1994

APPENDIX A

Mexican National Household Income Expenditure Survey (ENIGH)

The data used are from the Mexican National Household Income Expenditure Survey (ENIGH) for 1984, 1989, 1992 and 1994. A consistent methodology has been maintained throughout the various years in order to ensure comparability across time. The surveys were carried out in the third trimester of each year.

The basic unit of analysis is the household, where the household is defined as a group of persons who share a common budget for food regardless of kinship relations. The household's surveyed were drawn from a multi-stage sample design with stratification. The samples ranged in size from 4,735 households in 1984 to 12,785 in 1994 (ENIGH, various years).

The households are divided into zones of high and low population density. Low density population zones are those areas with fewer than 2,500 inhabitants. High population density zones are those areas which meet at least one of the following criteria[1]: a) municipalities with at least one locality with more than 15,000 inhabitants; b) municipalities which are part of one of the twelve largest cities, a state capital, or any other city over 100,000; c) other urban areas with a population between 2,500 and 99,999 (INEGI, various years). In this paper, I will use the high and low density zones as rough proxies for urban and rural areas.

As designed the samples are representative for both urban and rural areas at the national level. In addition, as will be illustrated in the following section, when a large enough confidence interval is allowed, the samples are representative at the sub-national level and may be used for regional analysis.

APPENDIX B

Adjustments to Account for Changes in the Price Level

The reference period for the reporting of household expenditure varies considerably by the type of expenditure. The reference period for expenditures on food, beverages and tobacco, for instance, is the week during which the survey was administered, while the reference period for expenditures on durable goods is the six months prior to the month in which the survey was administered. This characteristic of the data implies that inflating the different components of total household expenditure by the same factor may distort the picture of household expenditure, exaggerating the weight of expenditures on items with short reference periods which must necessarily have been purchased close to the survey date relative to expenditures on items with long reference periods which may have been purchased as much as six months before the survey date. For this reason, each component of total household expenditure should be deflated to the midpoint of its reference period before the components are summed. Unfortunately, the form in which INEGI releases the data does not permit total expenditure to be deflated by each component. Since the bulk of expenditures of the poor tend to be on items with the shortest reference period, in this study, total household expenditure is deflated to the midpoint of the shortest reference period.

Within each survey year, the extreme poverty line is adjusted for the differences in survey date by using the CPI for households with income equivalent to less than one minimum wage. The moderate poverty line is adjusted using the CPI for households with income between one and three minimum wages. The average income for households in these income groups is quite close to the poverty lines being used: the average income for households which earn less than one minimum wage is roughly eight percent higher than the extreme poverty line for urban households, and the average income for households earning between one and three minimum wages is nine percent higher than the moderate poverty line for urban households. These income specific CPIs were calculated based on the consumption bundles reported by these income groups in the 1977 income-expenditure survey. During the adjustment period, these indices have increased more slowly than the general CPI, and should better reflect the effect of inflation on the purchases of the poor.

APPENDIX C

Testing for Statistical Significance

Because the poverty rates above are estimated from data derived from a sample survey, it cannot be assumed that observed differences in poverty rates estimated from survey data reflect actual changes in the poverty rates of the underlying population. Observed differences may simply reflect errors in sampling. In order to test for the statistical significance of changes in the poverty rates, I have used a significance test based on Kakwani's (1990) derivation of the asymptotic distributions for poverty measures.

In general, for data generated from simple random sampling, a test for the significance of observed changes in poverty is given by:

$$ t = \frac{\left(\hat{P_1} - \hat{P_2} \right)}{SE\left(\hat{P_1} - \hat{P_2} \right)} $$

where

$$ SE\left(\hat{P_1} - \hat{P_2} \right) = \left(\frac{\hat{\sigma}_1^2}{n_1} + \frac{\hat{\sigma}_2^2}{n_2} \right)^{\frac{1}{2}} $$

and

$$ \hat{\sigma}^2 = \left[\frac{1}{n} \sum_{i=1}^{q} \left(\frac{Z - Y_i}{Z} \right)^{2\alpha} \right] - \left[\frac{1}{n} \sum_{i=1}^{q} \left(\frac{Z - Y_i}{Z} \right)^{\alpha} \right]^2 $$

Where $\hat{P}_i$ are the estimates for poverty measures P_1 and P_2, $\hat{\sigma}_i^2$ are the sample estimators of the variance, n_1 and n_2 are the sizes of independently drawn samples, Y_i is the income of the ith household and $\overline{Y}$ is the mean household income.

It is important to note, however, that the data from the ENIGH are not drawn from a simple random sample, but rather from a complex multi-staged sample. The clustering in the ENIGH sample frame reduces the effective sample size. The reduced effective sample size implies that estimates of the standard error will be too large if the design effect is not accounted for. This implies that the use of a test statistic calculated using the unadjusted standard error may lead to inaccurate inferences - the probability of type one errors is increased. In order to accurately estimate the standard error, the design effect of the sample frame must be taken into account. When we account for the design effect the adjusted standard error becomes:

$$SE\left(\hat{P}_1 - \hat{P}_2\right) = \left(\frac{\hat{\sigma}_1^2}{n_1}d_1 + \frac{\hat{\sigma}_2^2}{n_2}d_2\right)^{\frac{1}{2}}$$

where $d_i = \rho(v-1)+1$, $i=1,2$ and where d_i is the design effect for the ith sample, ρ is the intraclass correlation coefficient, and v is the average number of households per cluster.

APPENDIX D

Table 4.A.1: **Test Statistics for Changes in Poverty Rates**

		HEAD COUNT	POVERTY GAP	FGT
EXTREME POVERTY				
1984-1989	Rural	-5.08*	-5.08*	-6.00*
	Urban	0.52	0.95	0.71
	National	-2.33*	-2.40*	-2.92*
1989-1992	Rural	2.91*	3.60*	11.00*
	Urban	2.71*	1.82	2.50*
	National	2.10*	1.19	1.76+
1992-1994	Rural	-0.50	1.04	3.53*
	Urban	1.17	-1.00	0.00
	National	-0.31	0.67	1.43
1984-1994	Rural	-3.17*	-1.20	-0.37
	Urban	1.82+	1.67	2.50*
	National	-1.65	-1.04	-0.83+

Table 4.A.1:   Continued

MODERATE POVERTY		HEAD COUNT	POVERTY GAP	FGT
1984-1989	Rural	-4.60*	-2.29*	-5.16*
	Urban	2.71*	2.42*	2.92*
	National	0.54	0.50	0.24
1989-1992	Rural	3.00*	3.40*	9.70*
	Urban	3.58*	3.40*	5.78*
	National	3.00*	2.09*	3.85*
1992-1994	Rural	-1.40	-0.91	-1.67+
	Urban	-1.33	-0.50	-0.69
	National	-1.60	-0.50	-0.40
1984-1994	Rural	-3.66*	-1.15	-0.81
	Urban	6.07*	4.30*	12.5
	National	1.50	1.60	3.33*

Source: Author's calculations from ENIGH, various years.
Note: Asterisks indicate changes which are significant at the 5% confidence level

Notes

1   See Foster (1984) for a broad review.
2   See Srinivasan, 1981.
3   Errors in the household weights included in the ENIGH data sets for 1992 and 1994 make it impossible to expand the raw data by the appropriate weights for these years. In order to allow for comparison among the results of the different surveys, the calculation of poverty rates for all four survey years was performed without weighting the data. For the data sets for which the correct weights are provided, i.e. 1984 and 1989, the differences in poverty rates calculated using the weighted and unweighted data are slight.
4   Appendix A provides details on the ENIGH data.
5   Although some adjustments were made to allow for differences in the rural and urban consumption bundles, the differences are slight.
6   COPLAMAR actually constructed fifteen different food baskets which met the basic nutritional requirements, but which varied in the number and proportion of food items included. The basket which was chosen was not the least cost bundle, but exceeded the minimum by 36 per cent (Levy).
7   Levy (1991) points out that Streeten (1989a) and Lipton (1988) have presented evidence indicating that these irreducible expenditures are equivalent to approximately twenty percent the value of the minimum expenditure bundle; this implies a scaling factor of 1.25.
8   It is often argued that the lower costs associated with food in rural areas imply that a lower poverty line should be used for rural areas (Altimir). In this study, a single poverty line has been used for both rural and urban areas. The reasons are two fold. First, in Mexico large subsidies for urban consumers of basic foods like tortillas and milk decrease the difference which may exist between rural and urban food costs. Second, as noted in Appendix A, households in the ENIGH survey are not divided into precise rural and urban categories. Rather, they are divided into areas of low and high population density. While the definitions of rural and urban must necessarily be arbitrary in any study, it is not clear in this context to what extent the pattern of prices in low/high density population areas will correspond to the pattern of price differentials observed between rural and urban areas.
9   The value of the moderate poverty line includes the cost of certain items, like expenditure on culture, which may not be universally accepted as necessary for the meeting of basic needs. However, in order to allow for comparison with other studies of poverty in Mexico which have used this poverty line, and to avoid the task of trying to independently determine the appropriate composition of a bundle which meets basic needs, the value of the CNSE, which defines the value of a basket meeting basic needs as defined by the Mexican government, will be used as the moderate poverty line in this study.
10 The extreme poverty lines were inflated using the CPI for households with income equivalent to less than one minimum wage. The moderate poverty

lines were inflated using the CPI for households earning between one and three minimum wages. Appendix B provides greater detail on the adjustments made to the data to account for inflation.

[11] See Appendix C for a discussion of the statistical significance of changes in the poverty rates.

[12] See Khan (1996) for a discussion of the relationship between growth and poverty in the context of China.

[13] Alarcon (1994) inflated the extreme poverty line using the food price index of the Banco de Mexico, and in order to adjust the moderate poverty line the "appropriate commodity price index" was used to "calculate the value of each component on the CNSE based on the prices prevailing when the households were surveyed". Ideally, the poverty lines for different years should be calculated based on both price *and* consumption data for each survey year. Inferences about changes in poverty over time which rely on a single poverty line which is inflated by the CPI for use in various years ignore the effect of relative price changes on the consumption patterns of the poor. As the relative price of goods within their consumption bundle increases, the poor will tend to substitute away from these goods. Thus, depending on the price elasticity of these goods, the cost of the basket of goods purchased to meet their basic needs will tend to increase less quickly than the general price level. Given this, merely inflating the value of the poverty line by the CPI will not accurately reflect changes in the true cost of the consumption bundle necessary to meet basic needs, and estimates of poverty based on these price adjustments will tend to overstate the poverty rate.

[14] 1984 prices.

[15] 1984 prices.

[16] 1989 prices.

[17] It should be noted, however, that the effect on the rate of poverty of a shift in the income distribution cannot be determined *a priori;* for example, a large transfer of income from a household slightly above the poverty line to a household far below it will decrease inequality, but will increase the extent of poverty.

[18] The technique used here to decompose the changes in poverty is based on a technique developed by Kakwani (1990).

[19] The Lorenz Curve is a graphical representation of the relationship between the cumulative distribution of households ordered by income (expenditure) level and the size distribution of income (expenditure).

[20] It may seem surprising that the redistribution effect accentuated the fall in poverty at a time when income inequality as measured by the Gini coefficient was basically unchanged (Fujii and Aguilar). However, again it must be stressed that it is changes in the distribution near the poverty line which are the most important. Table 4.10 reveals an apparent improvement in the distribution in the lower deciles.

5 Adjustment Policies and Poverty in Mexico

The results for the measurement of poverty reported in the previous chapter indicate that the adjustment process did not lead to a reduction in poverty. At the national level, the number of poor increased over both the short run period from 1984 to 1989 and the longer run period from 1984 to 1994. There were, however, important differences between the performance of the rural and urban sectors, with the poverty rates in rural areas increasing and poverty rates in urban areas decreasing.

This chapter will examine the causes of the changes in poverty and the differing performances of rural and urban areas. It begins by examining how the key policy changes associated with adjustment affected poverty at the national level. It then examines the reasons for the differences in performance in different sectors.

Before examining how adjustment policies affected poverty in Mexico, it must be recognized that the increases in poverty were not due exclusively to the effects of the adjustment policies. Rather, the imbalances which created the need for adjustment, and the shocks which the economy sustained over the course of the adjustment period, also had deleterious effects of the poverty rate.

The likely effects of adjustment policies on the proximate causes of poverty, low wages and a lack of employment opportunities, were detailed in Chapter 2. In Chapter 2, it was argued that their complex and often contradictory effects make it difficult to anticipate *a priori* how poverty rates will respond to the implementation of a given set of adjustment policies. However, in examining the effects of an already implemented adjustment program, the observation of the responses of key variables to the adjustment policies allows some insight into how the policies affected poverty.

Among the components of a typical adjustment program with the potential for a strong impact on poverty rates, the most important are expenditure reduction and trade liberalization.

Expenditure Reduction

The policies to reduce public expenditure are designed to restore fiscal balance and curtail aggregate demand. They consist primarily of cuts in public investment and recurrent expenditures.

Public Investment

During the early period of adjustment in Mexico, there was a sharp decline in public investment (Table 5.1). Much has been made of the decrease in public investment over the adjustment period, but it is important to note that in the late 1980s, a surge in private investment began, which, by the early 1990s, had brought the rate of total gross capital formation back to the levels achieved in the oil boom years. After the initial stage of adjustment, total investment recovered quite well, but public investment continued at much lower levels. It is very likely that the initial dramatic fall in public investment aggravated poverty to some extent through its short run contractionary effect on the economy; however, to the extent that it decreased the economy's long run capacity for growth and job creation, it is likely that its long run effect will be greater.

It is too early to discern what the precise long run effect on wages and employment of the reduced investment during this period will be. However, given that the decline in public investment has caused a severe deterioration in the nation's infrastructure, there will certainly be some negative effect.[1]

In addition to the shift in importance from public to private investment, the nature of the foreign capital inflows has also changed. In the 1980s, portfolio equity investments were non-existent in Mexico, but by 1993, they accounted for over two thirds of all foreign investment (Oks and van Wijnbergen). *Ceteris paribus* any increase in a nation's capital stock should be advantageous, but this shift to portfolio investment may not be as effective in stimulating long run wage and employment growth. Because portfolio investment is not accompanied by the same sort of technology transfer as direct foreign investment, portfolio investment may not be as successful in increasing productivity, and hence wage levels; and because portfolio investment can be withdrawn relatively quickly, as it was in the peso crisis in 1994, it may not be as effective in stimulating stable long run growth.

Recurrent Expenditure

The most important cuts in recurrent expenditure came from decreases in the wages of public sector employees. These cuts came as part of a broader strategy of wage suppression designed to deflate domestic demand. Public sector wages and the minimum wage were allowed to fall in real terms. The decline in the value of the minimum wage was of particular importance.[2] Although relatively few workers actually earn the minimum wage in Mexico, it is important in determining wage rates throughout the economy because many wages, especially for unskilled labor, are set in reference to the minimum wage. In order to slow the inflationary pressure from increases in nominal wages, the nominal value of the minimum wage was set according to *ex ante* official projections of the inflation rate. The purported goal was to maintain constant the real value of the minimum wage. However, the actual inflation rates were much higher than the projected inflation rates used to set the nominal wage rate, and the real value of the minimum wage fell by over 40 per cent from 1980 to 1992 (ILO).

The decline in the minimum wage had a depressing effect on wages throughout the economy. Chart 5.1 reveals that average earnings fell dramatically in response to the wage policies and contraction in demand over the adjustment period.[3] From Chart 5.1 it can also be seen that the increase in poverty associated with the adjustment period was probably larger than that which could be measured given the available data.[4] Real average earnings plummeted by over 50 per cent in the first year of adjustment. In the following year they recovered just over half the lost value, but then declined again until 1988.

During the period of declining earnings from 1984 to 1988, there was also growing inequality among wage earners as the wages of unskilled laborers fell more rapidly than those of skilled workers. This explains, in part, why the increase in the incidence of poverty was accompanied by an increase in the severity and intensity of poverty. As real earnings began to increase again in 1988, the wages of skilled workers increased much more rapidly (Cragg and Epelbaum; McKinley and Alarcon). The relatively slow increase in the wages of low skill workers helps to explain why the increase in average wage levels between 1984 and 1994 did not result in a significant decrease in poverty.

The changes in wage structure during the adjustment period were accompanied by changes in the pattern of employment. Table 5.2 shows that the level of unemployment increased by approximately 50 per cent in response to the initial shock of the debt crisis in 1983. However, after 1983, the level of unemployment declined steadily through 1992, falling below even the levels of unemployment which existed during the oil boom before the debt crisis. The achievement of such low unemployment rates during a period of poor economic performance is all the more surprising because Mexico's labor force was growing by nearly one million persons a year over the period.[5]

The explanation for the surprising downward trend in unemployment can be found in the behavior of real wages over the adjustment period and the definition of employment which is used. The downward flexibility of real wages allowed firms faced with falling demand to reduce costs without decreasing the level of employment. It also allowed the government to reduce its expenses without having to dismiss workers. By accepting lower wages, many workers were able to remain employed throughout the adjustment period.

Of those workers who did lose their jobs, a large number found new employment in the informal sector. This shift in employment to the informal sector was quite substantial. Estimates vary, but it is believed that by the late 1980s, roughly a third of the work force was in the informal sector (Marcouiller *et al.*; Pastor and Wise).

The shift toward employment in the informal sector was accompanied by a number of other changes in the labor market which the unemployment rates do not capture. The difficulty with using the rate of open unemployment as an indicator of labor market health lies in the definition of employment used.[6] Persons are counted as employed if they have worked just one hour in the previous week or, even if they have not worked, they are counted as employed if they plan to return to work within a month. The lack of unemployment insurance and low wages in Mexico make it extremely costly for an individual to be unemployed. The phenomenon of remaining unemployed during a job search is a luxury which most Mexican workers cannot afford. As a result, during the economic stagnation which occurred during the 1980s, workers without the opportunity for well paid employment were willing to accept part time work, temporary employment, wages below the minimum wage, unpaid labor, and other such activities within the informal sector. Because of this flexibility within the labor market, the economy was able to create employment opportunities for virtually everyone in the work force. However, many of these opportunities tended to be lower paying and less secure jobs. The problem, in terms of poverty alleviation, was not with open unemployment, but rather with underemployment, the quality of the jobs created, and the wage level.

Liberalization

In Chapter 2, several reasons for the expectation that liberalization would reduce poverty were reviewed. In brief, the arguments for liberalization helping in poverty alleviation are that: a) according to the Heckscher-Ohlin model of international trade, freer trade should increase the relative wages of low skilled workers in developing countries; b) freer trade should result in efficiency and productivity gains which should stimulate growth; and c) the reversal of the discriminatory policies which placed agriculture at a disadvantage under ISI should increase the incomes of rural dwellers, who are typically among the poorest of the poor.

However, as we have seen in Chapter 3, liberalization did not lead to a significant reduction in poverty. In fact, as will be discussed later in this chapter, in the tradable goods industries whose workers should have benefited the most from liberalization, poverty actually increased.

There are several possible explanations for the fact that the predictions implied by the Heckscher-Ohlin model have not been realized. The first is that the opening of the economy has caused a rapid increase in the use of skill intensive manufacturing techniques. The massive increase in capital goods imports and the surge in FDI in the late 1980s have lead to an increase in the use of skill intensive equipment which requires skilled laborers. This trend toward more skill intensive technology has had important effects on the labor market - instead of low skill employment growing rapidly as predicted, employment in high skill jobs grew quickly and low skill employment grew much more slowly (Cragg and Epelbaum).

The second is that Mexico, along with many other middle income countries, is relatively well endowed with skilled labor by international standards, and its comparative advantage may no longer be in low skill labor intensive exports (ILO). Liberalization may, thus, cause a stronger increase in demand for skilled workers, who do not tend to be among the poorest members of the labor force, rather than unskilled workers, who do tend to be among the poorest members of the labor force.

In a series of case studies of electronics and automotive plants in Mexico, Shaiken (1990) has provided evidence of the ability of manufacturing firms to attract highly skilled labor and produce internationally competitive goods in industries which require relatively high skill labor inputs. Shaiken found that recently constructed plants have achieved productivity and quality levels comparable to similar American plants, but at much lower wage rates. Shaiken claims that the key to the success of the Mexican plants has been their ability to attract well educated and highly motivated workers. Shaiken's evidence lends support to the notion that Mexico's endowment of skilled labor is high compared to low income LDCs.

The third is that the recent surge in labor intensive exports from large low wage countries, most notably China, Indonesia and India, has intensified the long term decline in the terms of trade for these products.

In addition to removing the perceived biases against labor intensive industries, it was also expected that liberalization would reduce poverty by increasing efficiency and productivity. In a study of the manufacturing sector, Tybout and Westbrook (1995) found that average costs did decline and productivity did increase over the period from 1984 to 1990. As was discussed earlier, however, these improvements did not lead to a reduction in poverty in the short term. Indeed, one of the reasons for the improvement in efficiency, as measured by average costs by industry, is the reduction in real wage rates over this period. Given this definition of efficiency, short run improvements in efficiency and poverty alleviation will not necessarily be positively correlated. Whether or not the improved efficiency stimulates more rapid, sustained long term growth, which provides for a reduction in poverty, remains to be seen. The increases in efficiency and productivity are encouraging for the prospects of achieving faster growth, but shifts in the functional distribution of income toward profits and away from wages during the adjustment period suggests that the possibility of immiserating growth cannot be ignored.[7]

The final reason that liberalization may be expected to aid in poverty reduction was its anticipated effect on agriculture. However, the simple model which predicts that liberalization will tend to decrease rural poverty by improving the terms of trade for agriculture does not fit well with the Mexican experience. The terms of trade did improve for agriculture, but the conditions in which agriculture found itself at the start of adjustment made it vulnerable to the changes brought about by adjustment and, as will be discussed later in this chapter, poverty rates actually increased in the agricultural sector in response to the policy changes brought about by adjustment.

Changes in the Sectoral Distribution of Poverty

The results from Chapter 4 demonstrated that the changes in welfare which occurred during the adjustment period were quite different in urban and rural areas. While both extreme and moderate poverty rates were generally declining in urban areas over the period of study, in rural areas they showed a sharp increase from 1984 to 1989, and a smaller, but still significant, increase over the entire period of study. The dramatic difference in the trends in poverty in the urban and rural areas suggests that different sectors in the economy fared quite differently during adjustment. Most obviously, the relative deterioration of living standards in the rural areas would suggest that agriculture has performed poorly in comparison with the rest of the economy. In addition to the empirical evidence which suggests that agricultural households suffered disproportionately during adjustment, there are theoretical reasons to expect the adjustment process to have had differing effects on the welfare of individuals employed in different sectors of the economy.

As was discussed in Chapter 2, an important component of most adjustment programs is the implementation of policies designed to shift resources from the production of non-tradables to the production of tradables. In most adjustment programs, the most important policy tools used to bring about a shift in resources to the tradable goods sector is a sustained real devaluation. As the value of the domestic currency is lowered, resources should flow to industries producing export and import competing goods.[8]

This shifting of resources from one sector of the economy to another may have a significant impact on the employment and income of the poor. In fact, previous studies of the structural determinants of poverty in Latin America have demonstrated that the probability of being poor is indeed a function of not just the human capital and occupation of the worker, but also the sector of the economy in which the worker is employed (Rodriguez and Smith; Fiszbein and Psacharapolous). Moreover, in separate studies of the effect of adjustment on poverty in the Philippines and Indonesia, Balisacan (1995) and Huppi and Ravallion (1991) have found significant shifts in the sectoral distribution of poverty over the adjustment period.

Because labor mobility is low in the short run, the lower output and investment in sectors which are disadvantaged by adjustment policies means that adjustment will tend to have a disproportionately strong impact on the welfare of individuals employed in these sectors. This would suggest that in adjusting countries which succeed in shifting resources from the non-tradable to the tradable sector, individuals employed in the non-tradable sector would suffer disproportionately. However, expenditure switching is not the only policy change which may affect the distribution of poverty. In most adjusting countries, expenditure switching policies are carried out in conjunction with trade liberalization. Successful trade liberalization will expose industries in the tradable goods sector to competition. In the long run, this may lead to higher productivity and wages, but in the short run, previously protected firms are likely to fail in the face of more efficient competition; firm failure will cause a fall in employment and wages in the tradable goods sector. As such, in the short run, trade liberalization will tend to have the opposite effect of a sustained exchange rate devaluation, with the welfare loses associated with the liberalization component of an adjustment program tending to fall disproportionately on those employed in the tradable goods sector; whereas, in the long run, if greater efficiency is achieved as a result of increased international competition, the liberalization will tend to reinforce the effect of a sustained devaluation.

In this case, the distributional effect on poverty across sectors will be ambiguous in the short run, but will favor the tradable goods sector in the long run. However, the Mexican experience has been different from the standard adjustment process described above. While Mexico did undertake a program of trade liberalization, beginning in earnest in 1985, its exchange rate policies differed from the standard prescription of a sustained real devaluation.

As was detailed in Chapter 3, Mexico's adjustment process included a series of distinct stabilization plans. The first two stabilization plans, in 1982 and 1985, included sharp devaluations of the peso (Chart 3.1). However, rapid inflation returned after both of the plans and neither of the devaluations was sustained. Finally in 1987, the Mexican authorities instituted a heterodox stabilization plan which included a fixed exchange rate designed to act as an anchor for nominal prices. The exchange rate regime was later changed to a crawling peg. The stabilization plan was successful in slowing inflation, but Mexico's inflation rate still remained above those of its major trading partners. This meant that instead of a sustained real devaluation, the peso was actually revalued from 1987 to 1994, and by the early 1990s was at historically high rates. Thus, in contrast to the general case described above, in Mexico's case, stabilization policies would appear likely to have had disproportionately strong negative effect on the tradable goods sector in the short run and an ambiguous effect in the long run.

Head Count Ratios by Sector

In order to draw more sharply the distinctions between the tradable and non-tradable goods sectors, Tables 5.3 and 5.4 present the head count ratios for households grouped into the tradable, non-tradable and agricultural sectors.[9] The tradable goods sector includes the manufacturing and mining sectors. Of these two, the manufacturing sector is by far the larger, accounting for over ninety per cent of the production of tradable goods. The non-tradable goods sector includes the commerce, construction, transportation, finance and communal and social services sectors. The most important of these sectors are the commerce and communal and social services, which together account for over seventy per cent of the employment in non-tradables. Agriculture is reported separately because the average incomes are so much lower than in manufacturing and mining, and because traditionally heavy government intervention and a large subsistence sector cause it to behave differently than other tradable goods industries.

The results from the head count ratios estimated by sector of employment present a picture which is broadly consistent with the logit analysis. During the initial period of adjustment, from 1984 to 1989, and over the entire period of study, from 1984 to 1994, the extreme poverty head count ratio for households in the tradable goods and agriculture sectors increased by much more than the national rate (Tables 5.5 and 5.6). In contrast, while the extreme poverty rate for the non-tradable goods sector also increased over these two periods, it increased by less than the national rate.

The results for moderate poverty show a similar divergence in trend among the sectors. The moderate poverty rate for households in the tradable goods sector increased significantly from 1984 to 1989 and from 1984 to 1994, while the national poverty rate was experiencing a slight, but not significant, increase. The poverty rate for households in the agricultural sector also increased, though not significantly; with the agricultural poverty rate already so high, there was little scope for worsening. In contrast, the poverty rate for households in the non-tradable goods sector was decreasing over these periods, and it decreased by more than the national rate for both time periods.

Thus, the results the analysis by sector of occupation indicates that the performance in terms of poverty alleviation was quite different among the various sectors. The relatively poor performance of the tradable goods sector in the short run is consistent with the expected effect of the exchange rate and trade liberalization policies. The long run change suggests that the potentially positive effects of increased efficiency were not sufficient to overcome the deleterious effects associated with the real revaluation.

Tradable Goods Sector

For the tradable goods sector, painting with broad brushstrokes in this way yields a seemingly clear picture of adjustment's effect on poverty across sectors: the tradable goods sector performed relatively poorly in terms of poverty alleviation, and the obvious cause was the exchange rate policies which damaged the competitiveness of domestic tradables. However, an examination of other indicators of performance at the sectoral level reveals that the picture must be more complex.

Implicit in the argument that the revaluation of the peso would cause the tradable goods sector to perform relatively poorly in the alleviation of poverty is the assumption that the revaluation would hinder the growth of output, and therefore, employment and income, for industries producing tradable goods. However, for the periods from 1984 to 1989 and 1984 to 1994, output in the tradable goods sector actually grew much more quickly than for non-tradables or the economy as a whole (Table 5.7).[10] More importantly, the level of mean earnings for the tradable goods sector grew nearly 3 per cent from 1984 to 1989, while the economywide mean was falling by 9 per cent; and mean earnings grew by over 26 per cent from 1984 to 1994, while the economywide mean increased by only 6 per cent (Table 5.8). The fact that for both the periods from 1984 to 1989 and 1984 to 1994, the tradable goods sector experienced an increase in the extent of poverty at the same time the sector's mean earnings were increasing indicates that the simple model of exchange rate policies determining poverty rates through their influence on output does not accurately reflect the dynamic within the tradable goods sector.

It is surprising that an increase in the poverty rate should occur during a period of increasing output. Intuitively, a strong positive relationship between earnings growth and poverty alleviation would be expected. However, there is evidence from at least one other adjusting country that this positive relationship may not always hold. In a study of the effect of adjustment on poverty in Indonesia, Huppi and Ravallion (1991) found that the relationship between earnings growth and poverty alleviation across sectors was actually negative. This result is indicative of large shifts in the distribution of income within sectors.[11]

In Mexico, the static relationship between high mean earnings and low poverty rates does hold across sectors. Charts 5.2 and 5.3 plot each sector's head count index against its average earnings for each survey year. Not surprisingly, there is a strong negative relationship between the level of mean earnings and the incidence of poverty. Indeed, if the observations for the agriculture sector (the four observations with the highest poverty rates) were eliminated, the relationship would be very nearly linear. This negative relationship is quite similar for extreme and moderate poverty; the simple correlation coefficient for the extent of extreme poverty and mean earnings is -0.76 and for moderate poverty and mean earnings it is -0.72.

What is surprising, however, is that there is very little correlation between the rate of change in mean earnings and the rate of change in the incidence of poverty. The simple correlation coefficient between the rate of change in mean earnings and the poverty rate is only -0.18 for extreme poverty and -0.17 for moderate poverty. If the outliers for extreme poverty, all of which are from the mining and finance sectors which employ very few workers, are eliminated the correlation coefficient for extreme poverty actually becomes slightly positive.

The plots for the rate of change in mean earnings and the head count index demonstrate clearly that the strong negative relationship which was expected does not obtain (Charts 5.4 and 5.5). If the expected relationship between growth in earnings and the incidence of poverty held, the observations for the rate of change in these two variables in Charts 5.4 and 5.5 would fall exclusively in the second and fourth quadrants. Yet of the 27 data points relating the two rates of change, only slightly more than half fall in the expected quadrants - for a large proportion of the observations, poverty is either increasing as mean earnings rise, or, less commonly, decreasing as mean earnings fall.

The weak relationship between growth in earnings and poverty alleviation is particularly surprising in light of the results of the growth/equity decomposition in Chapter 4. The decomposition of the changes in the aggregate poverty rate into their growth and re-distribution components revealed that growth accounted for the majority of the change in the poverty rates. It appears that while growth is most important for poverty alleviation at the aggregate level, within sectors, changes in inequality play a much stronger role.

The manufacturing sector, which accounts for the great majority of employment and output in the tradable goods sector, is one of the sectors which experienced an increase in poverty at the same time its level of mean earnings was increasing. The explanation for this unexpected result appears to lie in the difference in performance between the larger, more capital intensive firms producing primarily for export, and the more labor intensive firms producing primarily for the domestic market. The import competing manufacturers were faced with a sharp reduction in domestic demand due to contractionary adjustment policies and, at the same time, trade liberalization exposed the previously protected industries to competition from low cost imported goods.

In contrast, export oriented firms benefited not only from cheaper capital and intermediate goods as a result of trade liberalization and exchange rate appreciation, but were also assisted by the aggressive promotion of manufactured exports by the government. In addition to the already existing *maquiladora* program, in the mid-1980s, the government adopted two new programs designed to stimulate manufactured exports. The PITEX program eliminated duties on the import of goods to be used as inputs in the production of exports, and the ALTEX program was designed to cut red tape by easing customs clearance and the reimbursement of the value added tax, as well as improving access to trade information for export-oriented firms. In addition, special export promotion programs were also instituted for several key export industries, including the automotive, computer and pharmaceutical industries.

Manufacturing exports responded strongly to the shift in incentives caused by these policies. The share of manufactured goods in total exports increased from just 17 per cent in 1982 to nearly 70 per cent in 1994. Within the manufacturing sector, export-oriented industries grew more rapidly than the "traditional labor-intensive" industries which produced primarily for the domestic market (Peters). It is important to note that the successful export-oriented industries tended to be more capital-intensive than those high cost import-substituting industries which were not successful in an environment of increased competition from imports (United Nations, 1992). Table 5.9 lists the industries which achieved the fastest and slowest growth in the manufacturing sector from 1987 through 1993. In addition to the concentration of export-oriented industries in the faster growing group, it can also be seen that the faster growing industries were relatively capital intensive: the average capital-intensity of the best performing industries was nearly twice the sector average, while the average capital intensity of the worst performing industries was only two thirds the industry average.

This shift within the manufacturing sector, in which the most dynamic industries were export oriented and relatively capital intensive, is important for explaining why an increase in average earnings in the sector failed to decrease poverty. Two important changes in the labor market were associated with this shift. First, the concentration of growth among relatively capital intensive industries did not result in rapid employment growth. In fact, if the entire period from 1984 to 1994 is considered, employment in the manufacturing sector actually shrank (Table 5.10)[12].

Second, there was a shift in the type of labor employed. In an examination of input utilization in Mexican industries, Cragg and Epelbaum (1996) showed that capital has a different relation with different types of labor. They suggest that while capital and unskilled labor are substitutes, capital and skilled labor are complements. Their argument is supported by separate studies using plant level data by Bernard and Revenga (cited in Cragg and Epelbaum), which found that more capital intensive plants hire a higher proportion of skilled workers and offer higher wages.

The faster growth of the relatively capital intensive manufacturing industries and the complementarity between capital and skilled labor were reflected in the labor market during the adjustment period. From 1987 to 1993 the growth in employment for skilled laborers grew at over four times the rate of the growth in employment of unskilled workers (Cragg and Epelbaum). The relatively rapid growth in skilled employment and the relatively inelastic supply of skilled labor also caused the wages of skilled workers to rise much more rapidly than the wages of unskilled workers. The more rapid growth in the wages of skilled laborers resulted in an increase in wage dispersion among manufacturing workers. This increase in inequality which resulted from the increased wage dispersion and the slow growth of employment opportunities for low skill workers explain why the increase in average earnings in the sector failed to alleviate poverty. It appears that the relatively rapid growth of capital intensive manufacturing industries caused growth in wages and employment to be concentrated not among unskilled workers who are at greatest risk of poverty, but rather among the relatively high income skilled workers.

Agriculture Sector

Over the period of study, adjustment policies did not lead to a decline in poverty among households employed in the agriculture sector. Instead, there were large increases in the number of poor and the proportion of households in poverty over both the short and long run.

At first blush it would seem that, as part of the tradable goods sector, agriculture would be favored by adjustment. In import substituting economies, agriculture is frequently disadvantaged by policies which re-allocate resources to the urban manufacturing and service sectors; for example, overvalued exchange rates weaken the competitiveness of agricultural commodities in international markets and tariff and non-tariff barriers increase input costs. The removal of these policies during the adjustment process should stimulate growth in the agricultural sector and provide the opportunity for poverty reduction (Goldin and Winters).

However, it is also important to consider the effects of changes in the scope and nature of state intervention in the agricultural sector. Before adjustment, the level of state intervention was typically heavy in most LDCs, and liberalization of the agricultural sector has meant moving toward more market-oriented policies not only in international, but also domestic markets (Johnson). This is an important concern for the alleviation of poverty because the state interventions in agricultural markets frequently have specific income objectives. In cases where the benefits of state intervention are captured primarily by relatively prosperous farmers, the distributional impact of their elimination may be positive. In cases where state interventions are designed to support the incomes of relatively poor producers of less competitive crops, liberalization is likely to worsen poverty.

As was discussed in the previous section, one of the presumed advantages of adjustment for agriculture, the devaluation of the exchange rate, was not achieved in Mexico. After two devaluations in the early stages of adjustment, the peso was allowed to appreciate to historically high levels. Because of Mexico's move toward a more heterodox adjustment strategy, any of the advantages for the sector associated with a more competitive peso were limited to the first few years of adjustment.

In order to understand the scope of the state's role in the agricultural sector, it is instructive to review briefly the agricultural strategies which were followed during the ISI period before adjustment.

The period from 1940 to 1955 was one of rapid growth for the agricultural sector. In the post war years, Mexico embarked on an agricultural strategy which included elaborate planning, the control of the pattern of production by tying credit and other input subsidies to specific production packages, the provision of guarantee prices intended to increase the incomes of producers of basic grains, and large scale public investment in rural infrastructure. The state hoped that by stimulating rapid agricultural growth, food prices, and hence urban labor costs, could be kept low. The increase in investment and subsidies and the continuation of land reform was successful in stimulating the sector. Agricultural production grew by 5.5 per cent a year over the period, and self-sufficiency in basic food crops was achieved (Rello).

The increases in rural income associated with this rapid growth were important to the import substitution strategy as they helped to expand the market for domestically produced manufactured goods. However, the benefits of rapid growth in the sector were not distributed equally. Most of the benefits of heavy public investment in irrigation and roads were captured by relatively large producers and the polarization of the agricultural sector increased. In 1950, infrasubsistence holdings, defined as those whose production was insufficient to provide for the household's basic needs, accounted for roughly half the cultivated land, but contributed only 6 per cent of agricultural production; while the category of the largest and most highly capitalized farms accounted for only 0.3 per cent of the cultivated land, but produced a quarter of agricultural output (Rello). By 1960, the contribution of the infrasubsistence farms had fallen to 4 per cent of total agricultural output, while the contribution of the largest farms had increased to 32 per cent.

After this initial period of rapid growth, advances in the agricultural sector slowed. From 1955 to 1972, output growth averaged just 3 per cent a year and declined dramatically in the late 1960s and early 1970s (Villa-Issa). The growing inflationary pressure during this period caused a change in strategy which was largely responsible for the slower growth. The government's reluctance to dampen the incentives for rapid industrial growth meant that efforts to slow inflation through price restraint were concentrated on agricultural goods. Prices for basic agricultural goods were allowed to decline by nearly 20 per cent in real terms.

In response to the fall in agricultural prices and the negative protection of the sector due to the overvalued exchange rate, private investment, which had grown rapidly in the previous period, stagnated. Public investment, in contrast, continued to grow rapidly. The balance of agricultural investment, therefore, shifted heavily toward the public sector. At the same time, the nature of public investment also shifted. In the previous period new investment in infrastructure had promoted rapid gains in the area under cultivation and crop yields, but the high cost of maintenance of these projects limited the scope for new projects; it is estimated that nearly one third of gross agricultural investment during this period was needed just to maintain or replace previously constructed irrigation systems (Villa-Issa).

The slowdown in agricultural growth and the rapidly expanding population meant that by the early 1970s Mexico was no longer self-sufficient in food. The need to begin large scale importation of basic grains occurred at a time of sharply increasing international prices. The expense of the agricultural imports, coupled with the mounting social pressure for poverty alleviation in the rural areas, led the government to shift its agricultural strategy once again. It was decided that the public sector needed to promote agricultural growth more actively. The government's response to the economy-wide stagnation at this time was expansionary fiscal policy, and the rate of public spending increased even more rapidly in agriculture than in the rest of the economy. From 1973 to 1982, net public investment in the agricultural sector exceeded 20 per cent of the sector's output, while from 1963 to 1972 it had been less than 10 per cent (Rello). The growth of subsidies was also enormous. The number of crops covered under a program of guarantee prices for key crops, which were typically well above international prices, was extended. The sector also became increasingly dependent on large input subsidies; for instance, the value of the subsidy on credit alone represented 10 per cent of the sector's output over the 1973 to 1982 period. By 1981 well over a quarter of all agricultural income was derived from public sector transfers (Rello).

Adjustment in Agriculture

The agricultural sector, thus, entered the adjustment period with a very strong dependence on the public sector. The legacy of the agricultural strategies followed during the ISI period was a sector with a tradition of highly centralized planning, a strong reliance on input and output subsidies, and a dependence on state financed rural development banks for the majority of its credit. The sector also relied heavily on public funds for investment because private investment was discouraged by the decreasing growth of productivity, the negative rates of effective protection caused by the overvalued exchange rate, and restrictions on private capital in the *ejido* sector.

The legacy of the agricultural strategies followed during the ISI period made the agricultural sector extremely vulnerable to the fiscal austerity and policy changes which occurred during adjustment. The changes which occurred in the agricultural sector during the adjustment period were similar to those in other sectors: the need for fiscal austerity implied a decrease in the flow of state funds to the sector, the shift in development strategy implied a decrease in the role of the state, and liberalization implied an opening of the sector. The agricultural strategy, thus, changed dramatically from the ISI period. Over the course of the adjustment period, agriculture became less regulated and more open to competition. The public sector's role in the provision of credit, commercialization of crops, determination of prices, and agricultural planning declined sharply.[13] In addition, the large subsidies for agricultural inputs, especially electricity, fuel and fertilizers, were reduced or eliminated.

The fiscal austerity which affected the entire economy during this period was especially harsh for the agricultural sector. The share of agricultural investment in total government investment fell from 17 per cent to 6 per cent between 1980 and 1989; in absolute terms, this was an 85 per cent real reduction in agricultural investment (Alarcon). The massive investment in rural development projects in previous decades implied high public expenditures for maintenance, repair, and replacement of the productive infrastructure and the severe decline in investment not only restricted the possibility for new investments, but also led to a deterioration of the existing infrastructure. By 1988, over 11,000 irrigation projects had fallen idle or partially idle due to a lack of funds for maintenance and repairs (SARH, cited in Rello).

The provision of credit to the sector also underwent important changes. Not only did the volume of agricultural credit decline by two thirds, but the interest rate subsidy on the credit still available, which had been quite large before adjustment, was virtually eliminated (Hewitt de Alcantara). In addition, the way in which the credit was channeled to producers was changed. Funds were shifted from public development agencies to private commercial banks.[14] This shift was a critical blow to peasant farmers whose relatively low profit margins and high risk exposure make them unattractive credit risks for commercial banks.

At the beginning of the adjustment period, many analysts warned that the reduction in spending and policy changes would result in a severe decline in agricultural production. However, the initial results were not the disaster which had been predicted. Instead, over the first years of adjustment, from 1983 to 1987, agricultural growth was slow, averaging approximately one per cent a year, but was actually faster than the economy as a whole. The relatively strong performance of the agricultural sector was due to the boost given to exports by the initial devaluation of the peso, a slight increase in the guarantee prices of basic grains, and favorable weather.

However, agriculture's relatively strong performance did not last. While the rest of the economy was beginning a recovery in 1988 and 1989, the agricultural sector suffered a severe contraction in output. The policies of exchange rate devaluation and favorable prices for basic crops which had initially mitigated the negative impact of adjustment were both reversed. The reversal of these policies, coupled with the effects of a severe drought caused agricultural output to fall by 6 per cent in 1988 and 1989.[15]

Adjustment's Short Run Effect

The slow growth during the early stage of adjustment and the sharp downturn in 1988 and 1989 meant that agricultural output fell by almost four per cent over the period spanned by the first two income-expenditure surveys (Table 5.7). Over this time period, average earnings in agriculture fell even more sharply than output (Table 5.10). Given that rural incomes are derived principally from agricultural production and the sale of labor power, it is not surprising then that poverty should have increased so rapidly over this period. And since the economy as a whole was growing, albeit slowly, and average earnings outside agriculture were falling much more slowly, it is not surprising that agriculture's poverty rate should have increased more rapidly than the poverty rates for the rest of the economy.

However, before concluding that, in the short run, adjustment caused agricultural poverty to increase dramatically on the basis of the evidence from the income-expenditure survey, several factors must be considered. The first and most obvious is that the data from the surveys provide information on only a limited number of years and not on trends in the evolution of the relevant variables. The limited number of data points provide a series of snapshots which may or may not be good indicators of the evolution of a dynamic situation. This is not to suggest that the surveys are not informative, but rather that it is important not to overstate the case for a trend by inferring too much from the limited data; in particular, caution must be used in concluding that adjustment's short run effect on agricultural workers was disastrous on the basis of data from just two agricultural seasons.

There is some reason to believe that the results of the 1989 survey may overstate to some extent the short run trend toward increasing poverty in the agricultural sector. As was mentioned above, agricultural income is derived principally from two sources: agricultural production and wages from the sale of labor power. While average earnings fell fairly steadily throughout the adjustment period, agricultural production did not. In fact, the level of agricultural production was quite erratic, and 1989 was much worse than the average performance over the adjustment period (Chart 5.6). This is not to suggest that the agricultural sector performed well with the exception of 1989. On the contrary, the growth rate was an anemic 0.8 per cent over the entire period of study. Rather, the point is that the results for 1989 reflect a poverty rate which is based, in part, on poor agricultural production which was a deviation from trend. The trend is admittedly poor, but not as bad as the 1989 production figures would suggest.[16]

The second reason for caution in interpreting these results relates to the way in which poverty is measured in this study. One of the apparent reasons for the increase in poverty in the agricultural sector in 1989 was the sudden fall in the guarantee prices for basic grains. Of the basic crops covered by the guarantee price program, maize is by far the most important. Indeed, it would be difficult to exaggerate the importance of maize for poor Mexican farmers. Maize is Mexico's most important crop in terms of area planted, employment creation, and value of production. In 1992, maize occupied nearly half of the arable land, including almost two thirds of the rain fed land and a quarter of the irrigated land (Appendini). Three fourths of all farms plant at least some maize. Maize production employs approximately one third of the rural labor force and two thirds of the workers involved in the production of Mexico's ten basic crops (Salcedo). In 1992, maize accounted for a fifth of the total value of agricultural production (Appendini).

Most of the maize in Mexico is produced by a very large number of small farmers on rain fed land; approximately 70 per cent of the maize is grown on rain fed land, and 90 per cent of it is produced by small farmers with less than five hectares of land (Appendini and Liverman). Most plots, particularly in the *ejido* sector, are of poor quality. The poor quality of the land in the *ejido* sector is reflected in low yields: the national average for Mexico is less than two tons per hectare, while in the American the average is seven tons per hectare. On average, maize production is not highly profitable. A study by the secretary of agriculture estimated that in 1988, only 65 per cent of maize producers were able to cover their costs of production. The same study estimated that less than eight per cent of the nation's maize producers could produce maize profitably at international prices (SARH, cited in Rello). It is important to note, however, that these national level estimates obscure the enormous diversity among maize producers. While most small scale farmers in the *ejido* sector produce at low or negative levels of profitability (when household labor and other inputs are valued at market rates), larger scale farmers who enjoy access to irrigation and other modern inputs earn large rents by producing maize which is sold at the high government support price.

Given the extreme importance of maize in the agricultural economy, it is easy to see why such a sharp fall in the price would cause poverty to increase. Again, rural incomes are derived primarily from agricultural production and wage labor. Assuming a simple factor share model of wage determination, it is easy to see that by decreasing the marginal value product of labor, a decline in the output price of maize would tend to drive real wages down.

However, the decrease in the maize price will also have a second, more direct effect on the perceived level of income and expenditure of rural households. A large fraction of agricultural production is grown for household consumption. This production is included in the calculation of income and expenditure, and is given a monetary value based on the relevant market price for the good. In the case of maize, the market price in rural areas follows closely the guarantee price, which fell by 25 per cent from 1984 to 1989. In the extreme, this implies that a subsistence household which produced only maize, would see its reported income and expenditure fall by 25 per cent even if it produced and consumed the exact same quantity of maize in 1984 and 1989. Of course, most households do not produce only for own consumption, but a significant fraction of maize production among the poor does go to own consumption. This artifice of the data collection implies that the large observed increase in the poverty rates among the rural poor may overstate the decrease in welfare suffered in households producing maize for own consumption.

The third reason for caution in attributing a large increase in poverty to the implementation of adjustment policies in the short run is the role of exogenous variables in determining the level of agricultural output. The most obvious of these is climatic variations. One of the reasons for the decline in output in 1988 and 1989 was adverse weather conditions.

While it is difficult to gauge to what extent climatic factors, and not agricultural policy, were responsible for the decline in production and increase in poverty in these years, the prolonged drought was clearly an important factor.

It should be noted that the severe drought which occurred during these years did not have an equal effect on all agricultural producers. Farmers with access to irrigation, who tend not to be among the poorest, did not suffer as acutely as farmers with access only to rain fed land. The worst effects of the drought were generally felt by the most disadvantaged farmers. This is an important factor to bear in mind when assessing the impact of adjustment, given that the results for the various poverty measures suggest that it was the poorest farmers who suffered most during the adjustment period.

Despite the need for caution in interpreting the survey results, the marked decline in public support for agriculture, followed by the sector's poor performance in terms of output, earnings and employment, suggest that adjustment did indeed result in an increase in poverty in the short run. Moreover, the fact that the decline in public support was more severe in agriculture than in other sectors, and that agriculture's performance was subsequently worse than the rest of the economy, suggest that it was the particular mix of adjustment policies followed which caused poverty rates to increase more rapidly in the agricultural sector over this time.

Adjustment's Long Run Effect

The results for the longer run period from 1984 to 1994 are very similar. Despite a slight shift in Mexico's internal terms of trade in favor of agriculture, the agricultural sector performed much worse than the rest of the economy. Over the entire period of study, agricultural growth was much slower and more erratic than the rest of the economy; average earnings fell by twice as much in the agricultural sector; and employment, which grew by 10 per cent in the economy as a whole, was stagnant in the agricultural sector.

The poor results at the aggregate level were compounded by unfavorable shifts in the incentive structure within the sector. The relative prices of the basic food crops grown by small farmers fell sharply in comparison to other agricultural products (Rello). The decline in the relative price of these basic food crops had a strong effect on poor farmers, whose ability to substitute to other crops in response to the shift in incentives is limited by their lack of access to key inputs, most notably irrigated land, credit, and information.[17]

In the future, the ability of poor farmers to react to falling prices in basic food crops will be critical for the future of poverty in rural Mexico. Of particular importance will be the elimination of the maize price subsidies, which have been called Mexico's "de facto rural employment and anti-poverty program" (Levy and van Wijnbergen, 1992). In the early 1990s, the price received by Mexican maize producers was still roughly double the international price. Yet under the terms of NAFTA, Mexico must eliminate the producer price subsidy to maize over a fifteen year period. The effect of the reduction in the producer prices on rural poverty will be partially offset by direct cash payments to small farmers for a time. The cash payments, however, will be phased out at the end of the transition period. As mentioned above, it will be difficult for many small farmers to make the transition to more profitable crops, at least in the short run, in the context of reduced public investment in agriculture. It is hoped that, as a partial solution to this problem, the changes made to the legal and institutional structures brought about by the Salinas administration in the run up to NAFTA will stimulate greater private investment in the sector. It is also hoped that job creation in the export sector will provide employment opportunities for those farmers who cannot adapt to the loss of the output subsidy. To date, the increases in private investment in agriculture and low skill employment opportunities in the export sector have been modest.

Conclusion

For the economy as a whole, the adjustment process did not lead to a significant reduction in the level of poverty. The expected benefits from liberalization either did not materialize or were dominated by the negative effects of the government's wage suppression policy and the stagnation of demand. The failure of liberalization to alleviate poverty appears to have multiple causes, including the shift toward more skill intensive manufacturing and the declining terms of trade of labor intensive exports.

The government's policy of wage suppression combined with these factors to force real wages down at the start of adjustment and keep them from recovering quickly over the period of study. The remarkable downward flexibility of wages helped to prevent the kind of massive job loss which occurred in other adjusting countries in Latin America, but a large portion of the growing work force was underemployed. The problem in terms of poverty alleviation was not open unemployment, but rather the decline in real wages and lack of growth in secure employment opportunities for low skill workers.

These effects of adjustment on poverty were not felt equally throughout the economy. The likelihood of falling into poverty varied by sector of employment, with the tradable and agricultural sectors performing relatively poorly. While the results from Chapter 4 indicate that growth is important for poverty alleviation at the aggregate level, there is surprisingly little correlation between growth in either output or earnings and poverty at the sectoral level. This suggests that there have been large shifts in the distribution of income within sectors over the adjustment period.

In the agricultural sector, the relatively large reduction in the level of state support appears to have been largely responsible for the increase in poverty. Before adjustment, the agriculture sector was heavily dependent on subsidies and public investment and management of the agricultural economy. The sharp decline in public support of the sector led to a decline in output growth and employment opportunities. The negative impact on the poor of the sector's poor performance was exacerbated by the reduction of producer price subsidies which caused the relative prices of the basic food crops on which the poor rely to decline.

Table 5.1:   Gross Capital Formation (billions of 1980 pesos)

Year	Public	Private	Total
1981	583.4	703.0	1,286.4
1982	473.6	596.8	1,070.4
1983	303.0	464.7	767.7
1984	315.4	501.6	817.0
1985	318.2	563.0	881.2
1986	272.9	504.3	777.2
1987	239.5	536.8	776.3
1988	229.3	591.8	821.1
1989	237.5	636.1	873.6
1990	267.8	720.4	988.2
1991	256.0	814.4	1,070.4
1992	243.3	943.2	1,186.5
1993	234.2	937.6	1,171.8
1994	255.0	1,012.0	1,267.0
1995	114.3	876.7	991.0

Source: La Economia Mexican en Cifras 1995.

Table 5.2: Open Urban Unemployment (percent of labor force)

Year	Rate	Year	Rate
1981	4.2	1988	3.5
1982	4.2	1989	3.0
1983	6.3	1990	2.7
1984	5.7	1991	2.7
1985	4.3	1992	2.8
1986	4.3	1993	3.4
1987	3.9	1994	3.7

Source: Lustig (1992) for 1981-1989; ILO (1996) for 1990-1994.

Table 5.3: Head Count Ratio for Extreme Poverty by Sector (head of household)

	1984	1989	1992	1994
Agriculture	.398	.452	.432	.429
Tradables	.087	.129	.100	.126
Non-Tradables	.089	.105	.094	.095

Source: Author's calculations based on ENIGH.

Table 5.4: Head Count Ratio for Moderate Poverty by Sector (head of household)

	1984	1989	1992	1994
Agriculture	.931	.938	.939	.938
Tradables	.699	.732	.701	.742
Non-Tradables	.741	.716	.668	.680

Source: Own calculations based on ENIGH.

Table 5.5: Change in Head Count Ratio for Extreme Poverty by Sector (head of household)

	1984-1989	1989-1992	1992-1994	1984-1994
Agriculture	.054*	-.020	-.003	.031*
Tradables	.042*	-.029*	.026*	.039*
Non-Tradables	.016	-.011	.001	.006

Source: Author's calculations based on ENIGH.

Table 5.6: Change in Head Count Ratio for Moderate Poverty by Sector (head of household)

	1984-1989	1989-1992	1992-1994	1984-1994
Agriculture	.007	.001	-.001	.007
Tradables	.033*	-.031*	.041*	.043*
Non-Tradables	-.025	-.048*	.012	-.061*

Source: Author's calculations based on ENIGH.

Table 5.7: Gross Domestic Product by Sector (billions of 1980 pesos)

	1980	1982	1984	1989	1992	1994	Cum. Change 1984-89	Cum Change 1984-94
Agric.	368	383	401	386	409	432	-3.8	7.6
Mining	144	179	182	183	193	198	0.6	8.7
Mfg.	989	1,024	991	1,135	1,281	1,317	14.6	32.9
Cons.	287	305	260	250	296	324	-3.7	24.4
Elec.	44	54	58	76	83	93	32.9	62.3
Comm.	1,250	1,370	1,267	1,302	1,464	1,485	0.3	14.4
Trans.	286	291	283	325	395	440	9.1	47.7
Finance	384	428	445	548	612	674	16.6	43.5
Com./ Soc Services	767	854	880	911	968	999	1.1	10.8
Trad.[a]	1,133	1,203	1,173	1,318	1,474	1,515	12.4	29.0
Non-Trad[b]	2,969	3,246	3,222	3,343	3,734	3,911	3.8	21.0
Total	4,470	4,832	4,796	5,047	5,616	5,857	5.2	22.1

[a] *Includes mining and manufacturing sectors.*
[b] *Includes construction, electricity, commerce, transportation, finance and communal and social service sectors.*
Source: Cuentas Nacionales de Mexico, various years.

Table 5.8: Average Earnings by Sector (thousands of 1980 pesos)

	1980	1982	1984	1989	1992	1994	Cum. Change 1984-89	Cum Change 1984-94
Agric.	17	16	14	11	10	9	-18.0	-32.4
Mining	145	133	105	98	101	92	-7.1	-12.2
Mfg.	133	133	107	110	130	133	4.0	24.5
Cons.	96	86	72	55	58	59	-23.0	-18.3
Elec.	296	311	210	180	207	221	-11.7	8.4
Comm.	82	74	63	52	53	55	-17.6	12.6
Trans.	111	107	94	90	91	90	-4.0	3.0
Finance	184	181	148	149	198	216	1.9	48.1
Com./Soc Services	95	98	78	70	83	89	10.8	13.2
Trad.[a]	134	133	106	110	128	129	2.8	20.9
Non-Trad[b]	97	95	78	68	77	81	-12.5	3.3
Total	79	79	64	58	66	68	-9.1	6.2

[a] *Includes mining and manufacturing sectors.*
[b] *Includes construction, electricity, commerce, transportation, finance and communal and social service sectors.*
Source: Cuentas Nacionales de Mexico, various years.

Table 5.9: Manufacturing Growth Rates by Industry

	Cumulative GDP Growth (1988-1992)	Capital Intensity (1988-1992)
High Growth Industries:	***11.2***	***0.43***
Automobiles	22.8	0.68
Fruits and Vegetables	11.3	0.06
Alcoholic Beverages	10.9	0.20
Basic Petrochemicals	9.6	2.11
Metal Furniture	9.0	0.09
Structural Metal Products	8.9	0.11
Electrical Equipment	8.8	0.16
Household Appliances	8.2	0.08
Low Growth Industries:	***3.66***	***0.14***
Tobacco	1.9	0.11
Paper and Paperboard	1.5	0.35
Corn Milling	1.3	0.02
Other wood products	0.8	0.02
Sugar	0.5	0.17
Wheat milling	0.3	0.05
Nonferrous metals	-0.3	0.19
Coffee	-1.0	0.24
Leather and footwear	-1.2	0.02
Lumber, plywood	-2.7	0.03
Cotton, wool, syn. Text.	-4.6	0.13
Pesticides and fert.	-7.4	0.42
Other trans. Equipment	-9.0	0.08
Jute, rough textiles	-31.4	0.49
Total	**3.6**	**0.22**

Note: High growth industries are those with cumulative growth rates exceeding eight percent; low growth industries are those with growth rates below two percent. Averages reported for these two groups are simple averages
Source: Adapted from Peters (1996).

Table 5.10: Total Employment by Sector (thousands of workers)

	1980	1982	1984	1989	1992	1994	Cum. Change 1984-89	Cum. Change 1984-94
Agric.	5,670	5,637	5,941	6,047	5,866	5,903	1.8	0.6
Mining	209	237	248	272	267	256	9.7	3.2
Mfg.	2,441	2,505	2,374	2,493	2,447	2,303	5.0	-3.0
Cons.	1,930	2,193	1,889	2,129	2,630	2,810	12.7	48.8
Elec.	81	89	94	109	111	108	16.0	14.9
Comm.	2,940	3,157	3,127	3,290	3,524	3,508	5.2	12.1
Trans.	904	1,037	1,006	1,025	1,132	1,148	1.9	14.1
Finance	352	426	465	490	507	522	5.4	12.3
Com./ Soc Services	5,723	6,201	6,338	6,476	6,734	6,895	2.2	8.8
Trad.[a]	2,650	2,742	2,622	2,765	2,714	2,559	5.5	-2.4
Non-Trad[b]	11,962	13,104	12,920	13,519	14,636	14,993	4.6	16.0
Total	20,283	21,483	21,483	22,331	23,216	23,455	3.9	9.2

[a] Includes mining and manufacturing sectors.
[b] Includes construction, electricity, commerce, transportation, finance and communal and social service sectors.
Source: Cuentas Nacionales de Mexico, various years

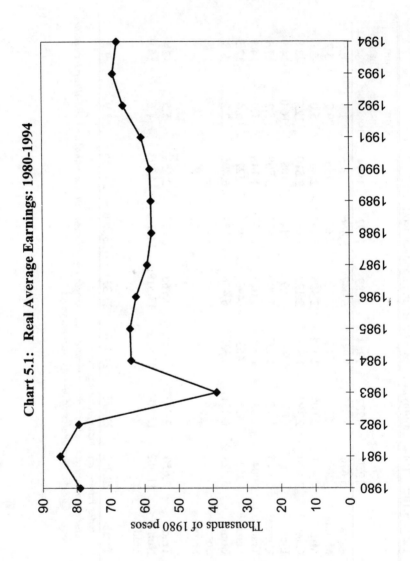

Chart 5.1:   Real Average Earnings: 1980-1994

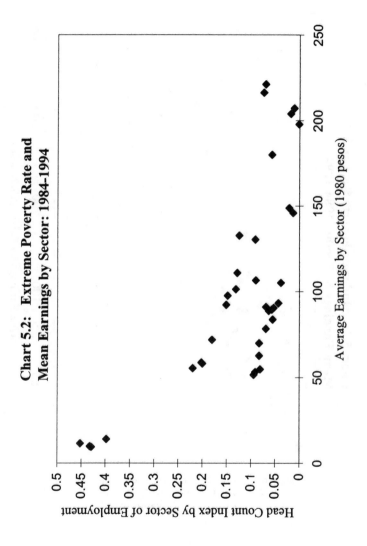

Chart 5.2: Extreme Poverty Rate and
Mean Earnings by Sector: 1984-1994

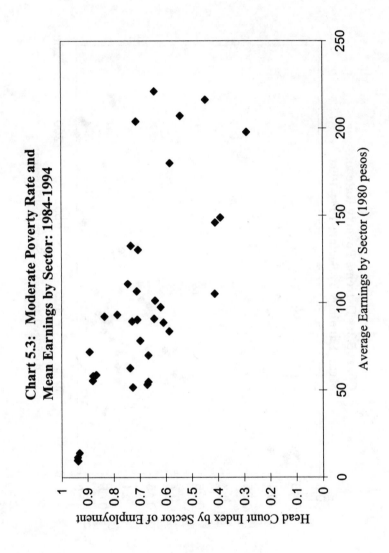

Chart 5.3: Moderate Poverty Rate and
Mean Earnings by Sector: 1984-1994

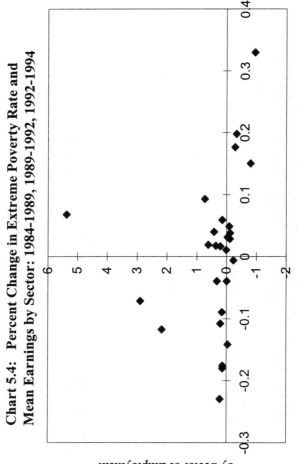

Chart 5.4: Percent Change in Extreme Poverty Rate and Mean Earnings by Sector: 1984-1989, 1989-1992, 1992-1994

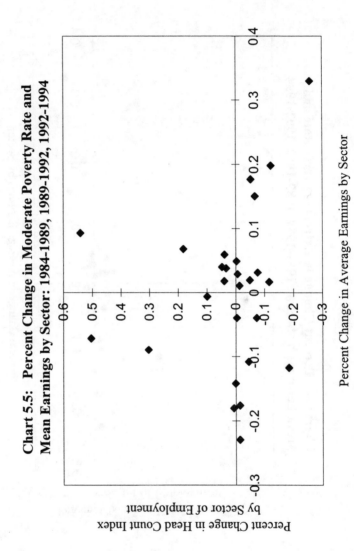

Chart 5.5: Percent Change in Moderate Poverty Rate and Mean Earnings by Sector: 1984-1989, 1989-1992, 1992-1994

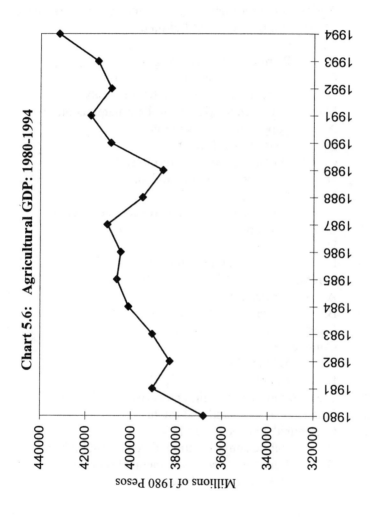

Chart 5.6:   Agricultural GDP: 1980-1994

APPENDIX A

Classification of Economic Activities

I.   Agriculture, Livestock, Hunting, Forestry and Fishing
II. Mining and Extraction of Petroleum
    A.   Coal
    B.   Petroleum and natural gas
    C.   Extraction of metallic minerals
    D.   Extraction of non-metallic minerals
III. Manufacturing industries (including maquiladoras)
    A.   Food, beverages and tobacco
    B.   Textiles and leather
    C.   Wood products and furniture
    D.   Paper products and publishing
    E.   Chemicals
    F.   Non-metallic minerals (except petroleum)
    G.   Industrial metals
    H.   Metals
    I.   Other manufacturing
IV. Utilities
    A.   Electricity
    B.   Water
V.   Construction
VI. Commerce
    A.   Wholesale
    B.   Retail
VII. Transportation and communications
VIII. Financial services and real estate
IX. Communal and social services
    A.   Public administration, defense, public health
    B.   Educational services, medical services
    C.   Restaurants and hotels

D.   Entertainment, culture, sports
E.   Professional and technical services
F.   Repair and maintenance services
G.   Agricultural, livestock, construction, transportation, finance and commercial services
H.   Services for international organizations

APPENDIX B

Table 5.A.1:   Test Statistics for Changes in Head Count Ratios by Sector

	EXTREME POVERTY				
	1984-1989	1989-1992	1992-1994	1984-1994
Agriculture	-3.50*	1.69	0.81	-2.63*
Tradables	-4.37*	3.77*	-3.47*	-5.60*
Non-Tradables	-1.78	1.52	-0.14	-0.88
	MODERATE POVERTY				
	1984-1989	1989-1992	1992-1994	1984-1994
Agriculture	-0.89	-0.02	0.02	-0.91
Tradables	-2.75*	2.82*	-3.81*	-3.07*
Non-Tradables	1.81	4.61*	-1.09	4.45*

Source: Author's calculations based on ENIGH..

Notes

[1] In response to the severe deterioration of its infrastructure, the Mexican government has sought to encourage private investment in infrastructure projects. To date it has enjoyed some success in attracting private capital to new infrastructure projects, particularly for road projects.

[2] Many authors have argued that minimum wages in LDCs may have negative effects on poverty alleviation because they are set too high relative to the average wage and, therefore, discourage employment in the formal sector (ILO). However, in a cross country analysis of developing countries, Lustig and McLeod (1996) have found that minimum wages are strongly associated with lower poverty rates.

[3] The average earnings reported in the Mexican National Accounts are not precisely equivalent to average wages. Earnings include the wages paid to all employees, including the wages paid to managers which may include part of firm profits (Alarcon, personal correspondence).

[4] The data from the income-expenditure surveys administered before the adjustment period began are not compatible with the ENIGH data used in this study.

[5] The rapid increase in Mexico's labor force was due primarily to the large number of young people in the population. However, the decline in wages during the adjustment period also increased the labor force participation rate as households increased the number of workers in order to maintain their standard of living.

[6] For a detailed discussion of the methodology used in the calculation of employment measures in Mexico see Rendon and Salas (1993).

[7] Alarcon (1994) provides a discussion of the shift in the functional distribution of income during the early stages of adjustment.

[8] Morley (1995) provides an interesting discussion of the importance of the size of the traded goods sector in determining how large a devaluation will be necessary and on the likely effects of a devaluation on producers and consumers.

[9] The head of household is used in this analysis because information on the sector of employment is not provided for all workers, but in most cases, only for the head of household in the ENIGH data set.

[10] The growth in the tradable goods sector was due primarily to the performance of the manufacturing sector, which grew by 33 per cent over the period of study, and not the mining sector which grew by just 9 per cent.

[11] Another possible explanation for the divergence in the trend between expenditures and incomes would be an increase in the savings rate. However, the savings rate in Mexico was actually falling over this period.

[12] The performance of the *maquiladora* sector in terms of job creation stands in marked contrast in the manufacturing sector as a whole. Employment growth in the *maquiladora* sector averaged almost 19 per cent a year from 1984 to

1989, and almost 13 per cent a year from 1984 to 1989 (Larudee). Originally the *maquiladora* firms were labor intensive operations whose labor forces had a high proportion of women. More recently, however, the program has attracted more sophisticated and capital intensive manufacturers of automobiles and electronics and has begun to hire a much larger proportion of men and skilled labor (Gereffi).

[13] Some indication of the extent to which the role of the state in the agricultural sector was reduced can be seen from the decline in the number of dependencies of the agricultural ministry, which fell from 94 in 1981 to just 20 in 1990 (Ibarra). Barkin and Taylor (1989) have suggested that the reduced size of the agricultural bureaucracy may have some positive effect by limiting the state's ability to dictate production projects to peasants - Gates (1996) has pointed out that many of these projects were of rather dubious profitability and were not free from political manipulation. Gates (1996) also argues that the elimination of corruption in the agricultural bureaucracy was one of the motivations for the shift away from a large role for the state in the agricultural sector. It is not surprising that a bureaucracy as vast as the one created to administer the state's agricultural policies suffered from some degree of corruption. However, Gates notes that the practice of falsely declaring crop failure in order to collect insurance benefits provided by the state was so widespread that the term *"industria de siniestros"* or "disaster industry" came into parlance to describe the practice.

[14] During the transition period before its elimination in 1991, Banrural, the main rural credit agency was re-structured to operate more like a commercial bank, financing only agricultural ventures with a high probability of earning a rate of return adequate to repay the loan. Previously, Banrural had acted more as a development agency, providing credit for use with specific technological packages which were often of dubious profitability (Gates). The perception of Banrural as more of a governmental development agency than a traditional lending institution hampered the bank's effectiveness. The default rate on Banrural loans was extremely high as credits issued by the bank were often treated more as transfers than as loans which required repayment.

[15] Lustig (1992) reports evidence that the decrease in production in these years may also have been due in part to a shortage of labor in the central agricultural states. The existence of a rural labor shortage seems surprising at a time of high urban unemployment, but the apparent cause was the large scale migration of labor to the United States. There is widespread evidence of heavy migration to the United States during this period, but it is interesting to note that according to the national accounts, total agricultural employment actually increased over the period. This discrepancy may be partially explained by the fact that migration to the United States is more a regional than a national phenomenon, with the vast majority of out migration occurring in the central agricultural states cited by Lustig as those suffering

from rural labor shortages.

16   It must be emphasized that even if the data for 1989 overstate to some degree the trend toward increasing poverty, the fact that poverty increased by so much in this year is important regardless of the trend. The loss of welfare in a single year will be particularly important for the poorest rural households who have little capacity for consumption smoothing and for whom any decline in nutritional intake could have very serious results. A decline in income which forces the selling of household capital or a decrease in the level of nutrition could have a lasting impact on the household's ability to recover.

17   Because there are important regional differences in Mexican agriculture, the shift in relative prices within the agricultural sector raises the possibility that there may have been regional differences in the evolution of poverty rates over the adjustment period. In general, a distinction may be made between the northern and central regions where access to irrigation, large markets, and transportation, storage and processing facilities is relatively good, and the southern region which does not enjoy these advantages. The infrastructure advantages of the northern and central regions makes these areas better suited for a variety of crops, while the southern region relies much more heavily on the production of basic grains and will find it relatively difficult to switch to new crops as the profitability of basic grains decreases. Unfortunately, the survey design of the ENIGH does not allow poverty rates to be estimated by region in order to determine if these differences in the capacity to switch crops have affected the evolution of poverty.

6 Conclusion

The adjustment policies which Mexico implemented during the 1980s and early 1990s were not successful in alleviating poverty. On the contrary, the absolute number of poor in Mexico increased over the adjustment period. This increase was sharpest during the early stage of adjustment, from 1984 to 1989, and it is likely that the observed increase in poverty from the period before adjustment to the early 1990s would have been even larger if data on household income and expenditure were available for the years before 1984. The increase in the number of poor at the national level is the result of a small increase in the rate of poverty in the context of a rapidly growing population.

The adjustment programs did succeed in bringing inflation under control, restoring fiscal balance, reversing the flow of capital out of the country, and changing the incentives governing production, but these changes did not translate into improved opportunities for the poor. Instead, real wages declined and there was little growth in well-paying employment opportunities for low skill workers.

The small increase in the poverty rate at the national level obscures substantial differences in the performance of different regions and sectors of the economy. The most notable difference is that the poverty rate increased in rural areas while declining in urban areas. The relatively poor performance of rural areas is not surprising given the poor performance of the agricultural sector. After performing slightly better than the economy as a whole for the first few years of adjustment, agricultural growth, real wages and employment declined sharply as the sector struggled to adjust to the reduction of state support. The increase in poverty among households employed in the agricultural sector is notable in that agriculturists are expected to benefit from standard adjustment programs. The explanation for the increase in poverty among Mexican agriculturists appears to lie in the extremely heavy dependence of pre-adjustment Mexican agriculture on public investment and subsidies, the decline in the producer prices of key crops cultivated by the poor, the revaluation of the exchange rate, and exogenous factors which include unfavorable weather.

Adjustment's effect on the non-agricultural tradable goods sector also failed to benefit the poor as expected. The sector did grow more quickly than the rest of the economy, but its performance in terms of poverty alleviation was actually worse. Instead of generating a large number of new jobs for low skill workers, most job growth came in more skilled employment positions. There are several possible explanations for this result; first, the opening of the economy caused a rapid increase in the use of more skill intensive technologies which required higher skill laborers; second, Mexico is relatively well-endowed with skilled labor by international standards and its comparative advantage may no longer be in low skill labor intensive exports; and third, the increase in labor intensive exports from other large low wage nations has accelerated the decline in the terms of trade for these products.

Although surprising, the relatively poor performance of the non-agricultural tradable goods sector in terms of poverty alleviation during this period of relatively strong growth in output and average earnings, was not unique. Over the adjustment period there was very little correlation across sectors between poverty alleviation and growth in either output or average earnings. The lack of a strong relationship between growth and poverty alleviation suggests that growth was accompanied by substantial increases in inequality within some sectors.

It may still be too early to judge the reforms' long term prospects for alleviating poverty, but the lack of progress to date does warrant some degree of pessimism. Despite the setbacks associated with the 1994 peso crisis, Mexico's fundamentals are in order once again - inflation is under control, and the fiscal and trade deficits have been corrected. Nevertheless, as several commentators on the Mexican reform have pointed out, the poor cannot eat fundamentals, and certain legacies of the adjustment process and the pattern of growth which has emerged in response to adjustment give reason for concern.

The cuts in spending on social services and the deterioration of the productive infrastructure raise questions about the economy's ability to generate sustained rapid growth. The long term effect of the cuts in spending on education and health services are difficult to predict and will not necessarily be severe. Many of the beneficiaries of these programs are higher income groups not at risk of poverty, and unlike many other Latin American countries, most of the decrease in public spending came at the expense of investment and not recurrent expenditure on social services. Nevertheless, there was a significant fall in real spending on education and other social services, and this trend is worrisome for an economy whose recent growth has been led by skill intensive industries.

The deterioration of Mexico's infrastructure, particularly in rural areas, is another potentially important obstacle to sustainable growth. There is a serious need to attract private capital or a renewed public commitment to at least maintain the existing infrastructure. Efforts to attract private capital to the financing of major new infrastructure projects, like road building, have had some success, but the strategy of attracting private capital to transform the countryside has shown little progress.

Even if these potential stumbling blocks to long term growth are avoided, there also exists the possibility that renewed growth will not be effective in alleviating poverty. The slow growth in real wages and employment apportunities for low skilled workers during the recovery of the late 1980s and early 1990s raises the possibility that the economy's response to adjusment may be a period of immiserating growth. The experience of the non-agricultural tradable goods sector, the most dynamic part of the economy during this period, was particularly troubling as poverty proved resilient to the sector's relatively rapid growth in output and productivity.

Even if the rest of the economy is able to sustain a pattern of equitable growth, there is also the danger that certain sectors will be left behind. In particular, trade liberalization and the elimination of many agricultural subsidies have raised questions about the viability of the traditional cropping patterns and production techniques of peasant agriculture. If profitable alternatives cannot be found for this segment of the rural population, which is already among the nation's poorest, the repercussions for rural poverty are likely to be quite severe. The declining profitability of traditional peasant agriculture is also likely to stimulate rural to urban migration, putting further pressure on the urban sector to produce additional employment opportunities for low skill workers.

Thus, although adjustment has helped bring about circumstances under which the economy can reasonably be expected to return to rapid growth, the legacies of adjustment are such that the realization of sustained growth and the ability of that growth to alleviate poverty are far from certain.

A good deal of caution must be used in drawing conclusions about the Mexican case which can be generalized to other countries, but several simple lessons of a general nature bear repeating. The first is that the strategy of using a fixed exchange rate as a nominal anchor to inflation may endanger long term growth, and hence poverty alleviation, by generating balance of payments disequilibria. The danger of running large balance of payment deficits in a context of highly mobile international capital was demonstrated by the peso crisis of 1994.

The second is that the liberalization of trade may not be as effective as hoped at increasing employment and income among the poor in middle income countries. In countries in whose comparative advantage is no longer in low skill labor intensive exports, and in which the poor are found primarily in household's headed by unskilled workers, liberalization may not be effective in creating the types of jobs which have the greatest impact on poverty.

The third is the danger of rapidly withdrawing public support from industries, like agriculture, which are heavily dependent on state support. When a compensating increase in private investment is not forthcoming, the poor in such industries will be especially vulnerable.

Bibliography

Adelman, Irma and Edward Taylor (1990), 'Is Structural Adjustment with a Human Face Possible?', *Journal of Development Studies*, 26(3):388-407.

Agénor, Pierre-Richard and Peter Montiel (1996), *Development Macroeconomics*, Princeton University Press, Princeton.

Alarcón, Diana (1994), *Changes in the Income Distribution in Mexico and Trade Liberalization*, El Colegio de la Frontera Norte, San Diego.

Altimir, Oscar (1982), 'La Distribución del Ingreso en México: 1950-1977', *Cuaderno 2*, Banco de México, México.

Amemiya, Takesi (1981), 'Qualitative Response Models: a Survey', *Journal of Economic Literature*, 19(4):1483-1536.

Appendini, Kirsten (1994), 'Agriculture and Farmers within NAFTA: a Mexican Perspective', in *Mexico and the North American Free Trade Agreement - Who Will Benefit?*, Victor Bulmer-Thomas, Nikki Craske and Mónica Serrano (eds.), St. Martin's Press, New York.

Appendini, Kirsten and Diana Liverman (1994), 'Agricultural Policy, Climate Change and Food Security in Mexico', *Food Policy*, 19(2):149-164.

Aspe, Pedro (1993), *Economic Transformation the Mexican Way*, The MIT Press, Cambridge.

Banco de Mexico (1997), *Short Term Economic Indicators*, Http://www.inegi.gob.mx/pubcoy/economy/prestab.htm.

Barkin, David and Edward Taylor (1993), 'Agriculture to the Rescue: a Solution to Binational Problems', in *Mexico and the United States: Neighbors in Crisis*, Daniel Aldrich and Lorenzo Meyer (eds.), The Borgo Press, San Bernadino.

Balisacan, Arsenio (1995), 'Anatomy of Poverty During Adjustment: The Case of the Philippines', *Economic Development and Cultural Change*, 44(1):33-62.

Behrman, J.R. and A. Deolalikar (1991), 'The Poor and the Social Sectors During a Period of Macroeconomic Adjustment: Empirical Evidence from Jamaica', *World Bank Economic Review*, 5(2):291-313.

Belausteguigoita, Juan (1992), 'Structural Adjustment and the Environment: Case Study for Mexico', in *Structural Adjustment and the Environment*, David Reed (ed.), Westview Press, Boulder.

Bourguignon, François, Jaime de Melo and Akiko Suwa (1991a), 'Modeling the Effects of Adjustment Programs on Income Distribution', *World Development*, 19(11):1537-1544.

Bourguignon, François, Jaime de Melo and Christian Morrisson (1991b), 'Poverty and Income Distribution During Adjustment: Issues and Evidence from the OECD Project', *World Development*, 19(11):1485-1508.

Calvo and Mendoza (1996), 'Petty Crime and Cruel Punishment: Lessons from the Mexican Debacle', *American Economic Review*, 86(2):170-175.

COPLAMAR (1985), *Las Necesidades Esenciales in México: Situación Actual y Perspectivas al Año 2000*, Siglo XXI, México.

Cragg, Michael and Mario Epelbaum (1996), 'Why Has Wage Dispersion Grown in Mexico? Is it the Incidence of Reforms of the Growing Demand for Skill?', *Journal of Development Economics*, 51(1):99-116.

Cornia, Giovanni (1987), 'Introduction', in Giovanni Cornia, Richard Jolly and Frances Stewart (eds.), *Adjustment with a Human Face*, Oxford University Press, New York.

Cramer, J.S. (1991), *The Logit Model: an Introduction for Economists*, Edward Arnold, London.

Demery, Lionel and Lyn Squire (1996), 'Macroeconomic Adjustment and Poverty in Africa: an Emerging Picture', *World Bank Research Observer*, 11(1):39-59.

Dornbusch, Rudiger (1992), 'The Case for Trade Liberalization in Developing Countries', *Journal of Economic Perspectives* 6(1):69-85.

Dornbusch, Rudiger and Alejandro Werner (1994), 'Mexico: Stabilization, Reform and No Growth', *Brookings Papers on Economic Activity*, 1(Spring):252-315.

Edwards, S. (1993), 'Openness, Trade Liberalization and Growth in Developing Countries', *Journal of Economic Literature*, 31(3):1358-1393.

Feinberg, Richard (1984), *Adjustment Crisis in the Third World*, Overseas Development Council, New Brunswick.

Fiszbein, Ariel and George Psacharpoloulos (1995), 'Income Inequality Trends in Latin America in the 1980s', in *Coping with Austerity: Poverty and Inequality in Latin America*, Nora Lustig (ed.), The Brookings Institution, Washington, DC.

Foster, J., J. Greer, E. Thorbecke (1984), 'A Class of Decomposable Poverty Measures', *Econometrica*, 52(3):761-766.

Friedman, Santiago, Nora Lustig and Arianna Legovini (1995), 'Mexico: Social Spending and Food Subsidies during Adjustment', in *Coping with Austerity: Poverty and Inequality in Latin America*, Nora Lustig (ed.), The Brookings Institution, Washington, DC.

Fujii, Gerardo and Genaro Aguilar (1995), 'La Distribución del Ingreso en México, 1984-1992: un Estudio por Componentes', *Comercio Exterior*, 45(8):609-614.

Gates, Marilyn (1996), 'In Default: Peasants, the Debt Crisis; and the Agriculture Challenge in Mexico', in Gerardo Otero (ed.), *Neoliberalism Revisited: Economic Restructuring and Mexico's Political Future*, Westview Press, Boulder.

Glewwe, Paul and Dennis de Tray (1991), 'The Poor in Latin America during Adjustment: a Case Study of Peru', *Economic Development and Cultural Change*, 40(1): 27-54.

Gereffi, Gary (1996), 'Mexico's 'Old' and 'New' Maquiladora Industries: Contrasting Approaches to North American Integration', in Gerardo Otero (ed.), *Neoliberalism Revisited: Economic Restructuring and Mexico's Political Future*, Westview Press, Boulder.

Gindling, T., and Albert Berry (1992), 'The Performance of the Labor Market During Recession and Structural Adjustment: Costa Rica in the 1980s', *World Development*, 20(11):1599-1616.

Goldin, Ian (1993), *Economic Reform, Trade and Agricultural Development*, St. Martin's Press, New York.

Goldin, Ian and Oden Knudsen (1990), 'The Implications of Agricultural Trade Liberalization for Developing Countries', in *Agricultural Trade Liberalization: Implications for Developing Countries*, Ian Goldin and Odin Knudsen (eds.), World Bank, Washington, DC.

Goldin, Ian and Alan Winters (1992), 'Open Economies, Structural Adjustment and Agriculture: Introduction: form Maize to Macro', in *Open Economies: Structural Adjustment and Agriculture*, Ian Goldina and Alan Winters (eds.), Cambridge University Press, New York.

Griffin, Keith (1996), 'Macroeconomic Reform and Employment: an Investment-Led Strategy of Structural Adjustment in Sub-Saharan Africa', Dept. of Economics Working Paper No. 23, University of California, Riverside.

Grootaert, Christiaan (1994), 'Poverty and Basic Needs Fulfillment in Africa During Structural Change: Evidence from Côte d'Ivoire', *World Development*, 22(10):1521-1534.

Gundersen, Craig George (1996), *Direct Measures of Poverty and Well-Being: a Theoretical Framework and an Application to Housing Poverty in the United State,* Doctoral Dissertation, University of California, Riverside.

Gurría, José (1995), 'Capital Flows: the Mexican Case', in *Coping with Capital Surges,* Ricardo Ffrench-Davis and Stephany Griffith-Jones (eds.), Lynne Rienner Publishers, Boulder.

Haddad, Lawrence, Lynn Brown, Andrea Richter and Lisa Smith (1995), 'The Gender Dimensions of Economic Adjustment Policies: Potential Interactions and Evidence to Date', *World Development,* 23(6):881-896.

Hewitt de Alcántara, Cynthia. 1992, 'Economic Restructuring and Rural Subsistence in Mexico: Maize and the Crisis of the 1980s', UNRISD Discussion Paper, Geneva.

Holt, Richard, and Linda Wilcox Young (1997), 'The Effects of Neo-Liberal Policies on Trade and Investment in Mexico', Paper prepared for Latin American Studies Association Congress, Guadalajar, Mexico, April, 1997.

Huppi, Monika and Martin Ravallion (1991), 'The Sectoral Structure of Poverty During an Adjustment Period: Evidence from Indonesia in the mid-1980s', *World Development,* 19(2):1653-1678.

Ibarra Niño, Carlos. 1993, 'Cambio estructural y potencialidades de crecimiento de la agricultura mexicana, 1982-1991', in *México: La Nueva Economía,* Julio López et al. (eds.), Nuevos Horizantes Editores, México.

INEGI (various years), *Católogos de Códigos: Encuesta Nacional de Ingreso-Gasto de Hogares,* INEGI, Aguascalientes.

INEGI (various years), *La Economía Mexicana in Cifras,* Nacional Financiero, México.

INEGI (various years), *Sistema de Cuentas Nacionales de México,* INEGI, Aguascalientes.

INEGI (1997), *Indicadores Económicos de Coyuntura,* Http//:dgcnesyp.inegi.gob.mx/cgi-win/bdi.exe.

International Labor Office (1996), *World Employment 1996/97: National Policies in a Global Context,* ILO, Geneva.

de Janvry, Alain, Elisabeth Sadoulet and André Fargeix (1991), 'Politically Feasible and Equitable Adjustment: Some Alternative for Ecuador', *World Development,* 19(11):1577-1594.

Kakwani, Nanak (1990), *Poverty and Economic Growth: with Application to Côte d'Ivoire*, Living Standards Measurement Study No. 63. World Bank, Washington, DC.

Kakwani, Nanak (1995), 'Structural Adjustment and Performance in Living Standards in Developing Countries', *Development and Change*, 26(3):469-502.

Kakwani, Nanak and K. Subbarao (1990), 'Rural Poverty and Its Alleviation in India', *Economic and Political Weekly*, 25(13):A2-A16.

Kennedy, Peter (1991), *A Guide to Econometrics*, The MIT Press, Cambridge.

Khan, Azizur Rahman (1993), *Structural Adjustment and Income Distribution: Issues and Experience*, ILO, Geneva.

Khan, Azizur Rahman (1996), 'Growth, Poverty and Globalization: the Impact of Recent Macroeconomic and Sectoral Changes on the Poor and Women in China', Unpublished manuscript.

Krissoff, Barry and Nicole Ballenger (1989), 'Agricultural Trade Liberalization in a Multisector World Model: Implications for Argentina, Brazil and Mexico', in *Government Intervention in Agriculture: Cause and Effect*, Bruce Greenshields and Margot Bellamy (eds.), Gower Publishing Company, Brookfield, VT.

La Economía Mexicana en Cifras (1995), Nacional Financiero, Mexico, DF.

Lamert, Sylvia, Harmut Schneider and Akiko Suwa (1991), 'Adjustment and Equity in Côte d'Ivoire: 1980-86', *World Development*, 19(11)1563-1576.

Larudee, Mehrene (1997), 'The Effects of Free Trade Agreements: Lessons from Mexico', Paper prepared for Latin American Studies Association Congress, Guadalajara, Mexico, April, 1997.

Levy, Santiago (1991), *Poverty Alleviation in Mexico*, Working Paper Series 679, World Bank, Washington, DC.

Levy, Santiago and Sweder van Wijnbergen (1992), *Agriculture in the Mexico-U.S. Free Trade Agreement*, Working Paper Series 967, Latin American and Caribbean Country Dept. World Bank, Washington, DC.

Lipton, M. (1988), 'The Poor and the Poorest: Some Interim Findings', World Bank Discussion Paper #25. World Bank, Washington, DC.

Lustig, Nora (1989), 'La Medición de Pobreza en México', *El Trimestre Económico* 59(4): 725-749.

Lustig, Nora (1992), *Mexico: the Remaking of an Economy*, The Brookings Institution, Washington, DC.

Lustig, Nora (1995), *Coping with Austerity: Poverty and Inequality in Latin America*, The Brookings Institution, Washington, DC.

Lustig, Nora and Darryl McLeod (1996), *Minimum Wages and Poverty in Developing Countries: Some Empirical Evidence*, Brooking Discussion Paper in International Economics, No. 125.

Lustig, Nora and Jaime Ros (1993), 'Mexico', in *The Rocky Road to Reform*, Lance Taylor (ed.), The MIT Press, Cambridge.

Magnitud y Evolución de Pobreza en México: Informe Metodológico (1993), INEGI, Aguascalientes.

Marcouiller, Douglas, Veronica Ruiz de Castilla and Christopher Woodruff (1997), 'Formal Measures of the Informal Sector Wage Gap in Mexico, El Salvador, and Peru', *Economic Development and Cultural Change*, 45(2):367-392.

McKinley, Terry and Diana Alarcón (1994), 'The Prevalence of Rural Poverty in Mexico', Unpublished manuscript.

de Melo, Jaime and Sherman Robinson (1982), 'Trade Adjustment Policies and Income Distribution in Three Archetype Developing Economies', *Journal of Development Economics*, 10(1):67-92.

Morley, Samuel (1995), 'Structural Adjustment and the Determinants of Poverty in Latin America', *Coping with Austerity: Poverty and Inequality in Latin America*, The Brookings Institution, Washington, DC.

Morrisson, Christian (1991), 'Foreword', *World Development*, 19(11):1633-1651.

Oks, Daniel and Sweder van Wijnbergen (1995), 'Mexico after the Debt Crisis: Is Growth Sustainable?', *Journal of Development Economics*, 47(1):155-178.

Orates, Guillermo (1994), 'Comment on Rudiger Dornbusch: Stabilization and Monetary Reform in Latin America', in *A Framework for Monetary Stability*, J. Wijnholds, S. Eijffinger and L. Hoogdiun (eds.), Kluwer Academic Publishers, Boston.

Pastor, Manuel and Michael Conroy (1995), 'Distributional Implications of Macroeconomic Policy: Theory and Applications to El Salvador', *World Development*, 23(12):2117-2131.

Pastor, Manuel and Gary Dymski (1990), 'Debt Crisis and Class Conflict in Latin America', *Review of Radical Political Economics*, 22(1):155-178.

Pastor, Manuel and Carol Wise (1996), 'Distribution, Social Policy and Neoliberal Reform in Mexico', Unpublished manuscript.

Peters, Enrique (1996), 'From Export Oriented to Import Oriented Industrialization: Changes in Mexico's Manufacturing Sector, 1988-1994', in Gerardo Otero (ed.), *Neoliberalism Revisited: Economic Restructuring and Mexico's Political Future*, Westview Press, Boulder.

Pozos Ponce, Fernando (1997), *Neoliberalismo y Política Salarial en México: Evidencias de un Política Irracional*, Paper prepared for Latin American Studies Association Congress, Guadalajar, Mexico, April, 1997.

Presler, Paul (1997), 'Stagnant Investment with No Growth: Mexican Neoliberal Reforms in the 1990s', Paper prepared for Latin American Studies Association Congress, Guadalajar, Mexico, April, 1997.

Ravallion, Martin and Guarav Datt (1991), *Growth and Redistribution Components of Changes in Poverty Measures: a Decomposition with Applications to Brazil and India in the 1980s*, Living Standards Measurement Study No. 83. World Bank, Washington, DC.

Ravallion, Martin and Monika Huppi (1991), 'Measuring Changes in Poverty: a Methodological Case Study of Indonesia during an Adjustment Period', *The World Bank Economic Review*, 5(1)57-82.

Rello, Fernando (1993), 'Adjuste Macroeconómico y Política Agrícola en México', in *México: Auge, Crisis y Ajuste*, C. Bazdresch, N. Bucay, S. Loaeza and N. Lusting (eds.), Fondo de Cultural Económico, Mexico, DF.

Rendón, Teresa and Carlos Salas (1993), 'El Empleo en México en los Ochenta: Tendencias y Cambios', *Comercio Exterior*, 43(8):717-730.

Rodriguez, Adrian and Stephen Smith (1994), 'A Comparison of Determinants of Urban, Rural and Farm Poverty in Costa Rica', *World Development*, 22(3):381-397.

Rosegrant, Mark (1990), 'Impact of Trade Liberalization in Indonesian Food Crops', in Bruce Greenshields and Margot Bellamy (eds.), Gower Publishing Company, Brookfield, VT.

Salcedo, Salomón, José Alberto García and Myriam Sagarnaga (1993), 'Política agrícola y maíz en México: hacia el libre comercio norteamericano', *Comercio Exterior*, 43(4):302-310.

Sen, Amartya (1973), *On Economic Inequality*, Oxford University Press, New York.

Shaiken, Harley (1990), *Mexico in the Global Economy: High Technology and Work Organization in Export Industries*, Center for US-Mexican Studies, San Diego.

Srinivasan, T. (1981), 'Malnutrition: Some Measurement and Policy Issues', *Journal of Development Economics,* 8(1):3-21.

Streeten, Paul (1989a), 'Poverty: Concepts and Measurement', Institute for Economic Development Discussion Paper #4, Boston University.

Streeten, Paul (1989b), 'A Survey of Issues and Options', in *Structural Adjustment and Agriculture: Theory and Practice in Africa and Latin America,* Simon Commander (ed.), Heinemann Educational Books, Inc, Portsmouth, NH.

Ten Kate, Adriaan (1992a), 'El Ajuste Estructural en México: Dos Historias Diferentes', *Comercio Exterior,* 42(6):520-527.

Ten Kate, Adriaan (1992b), 'Trade Liberalization and Economic Stabilization in Mexico: Lessons of Experience', *World Development,* 20(5):659-672.

Thorbecke, Erik (1991), 'Adjustment, Growth and Income Distribution in Indonesia', *World Development,* 19(11):1595-1614.

Tybout, James and M. Daniel Westbrook (1995), 'Trade Liberalization and the Dimensions of Efficiency Change in Mexican Manufacturing Industries', *Journal of International Economics,* 39(1):53-79.

United Nations Center on Transnational Corporations (1992), *Foreign Direct Investment and Restructuring in Mexico,* UMCTC Current Studies Series A, No. 8. United Nations, New York.

Villa-Issa, Manuel. 1990, 'Performance of Mexican Agriculture: the Effects of Economic and Agricultural Policies', *American Journal of Agricultural Economics,* 72(3):744-748.

Weiss, John (1992), 'Trade Liberalization in Mexico in the 1980s: Concepts, Measures and Short-Run Effects', *Weltwirtschaftliches Archiv,* 128(4):711-725.

World Bank (various years), *World Development Report,* Oxford University Press, New York.